ACAPULCO

Marc Rigole
Claude-Victor Langlois

ULYSSES
TRAVEL PUBLICATIONS
Travel better... enjoy more

Editorial *Series Director and Editor:* Claude Morneau; *Project Supervisor:* Pascale Couture.

Research and Composition *Authors:* Marc Rigole, Claude-Victor Langlois.

Production *Design:* Patrick Farei (Atoll Direction); *Editing:* Jennifer McMorran; *Translation:* Tracy Kendrick, Sarah Kresh; *Cartography:* André Duchesne, Steve Rioux (Assistant); *Layout:* Sarah Kresh.

Illustrations *Cover Photo:* Richard Heizen (Superstock); *Chapter Headings:* Jennifer McMorran; *Drawings:* Lorette Pierson.

Special Thanks to Guillermo Ponce (Mexican Tourist Office - Montreal), Piquis Rochin (Acapulco Tourism Board), Lillian M. De Lobato (Fondo Mixto de Promocíon Turística de Acapulco), J. Ramiro Reina A. (Elcano Acapulco), Elizabeth Gonzalez A. (Elcano Acapulco), Oscar A. Rivero E. (Days Inn Acapulco) and Karine Bouchard (Vacances Air Transat).

Thanks to SODEC (Québec government) and the Canadian Heritage Minister for their assistance.

Distributors

AUSTRALIA:
Little Hills Press
11/37-43 Alexander St.
Crows Nest NSW 2065
☎ (612) 437-6995
Fax: (612) 438-5762

BELGIUM AND LUXEMBOURG:
Vander
Vrijwilligerlaan 321
B-1150 Brussel
☎ (02) 762 98 04
Fax: (02) 762 06 62

CANADA:
Ulysses Books & Maps
4176 Saint-Denis
Montréal, Québec
H2W 2M5
☎ (514) 843-9882, ext.2232
Fax: 514-843-9448
www.ulysse.ca

GERMANY AND AUSTRIA:
Brettschneider
Fernreisebedarf
Feldfirchner Strasse 2
D-85551 Heimstetten
München
☎ 89-99 02 03 30
Fax: 89-99 02 03 31

GREAT BRITAIN AND IRELAND:
World Leisure Marketing
9 Downing Road
West Meadows, Derby
UK DE21 6HA
☎ 1 332 34 33 32
Fax: 1 332 34 04 64

ITALY:
Centro Cartografico del Riccio
Via di Soffiano 164/A
50143 Firenze
☎ (055) 71 33 33
Fax: (055) 71 63 50

NETHERLANDS:
Nilsson & Lamm
Pampuslaan 212-214
1380 AD Weesp (NL)
☎ 0294-465044
Fax: 0294-415054

SCANDINAVIA:
Scanvik
Esplanaden 8B
1263 Copenhagen K
DK
☎ (45) 33.12.77.66
Fax: (45) 33.91.28.82

SPAIN:
Altaïr
Balmes 69
E-08007 Barcelona
☎ 454 29 66
Fax: 451 25 59

SWITZERLAND:
OLF
P.O. Box 1061
CH-1701 Fribourg
☎ (026) 467.51.11
Fax: (026) 467.54.66

U.S.A.:
The Globe Pequot Press
6 Business Park Road
P.O. Box 833
Old Saybrook, CT 06475
☎ 1-800-243-0495
Fax: 1-800-820-2329

Other countries, contact Ulysses Books & Maps (Montréal), Fax: (514) 843-9448
Canadian Cataloguing in Publication see p 5

"One does not explain Mexico; one believes, with fury, passion and discouragement, in Mexico."

Carlos Fuentes

TABLE OF CONTENTS

Help make Ulysses Travel Guides even better!

The information contained in this guide was correct at press time. However, mistakes can slip in, omissions are always possible, places can disappear, etc. The authors and publisher hereby disclaim any liability for loss or damage resulting from omissions or errors.

We value your comments, corrections and suggestions, as they allow us to keep each guide up to date. The best contributions will be rewarded with a free book from Ulysses Travel Publications. All you have to do is write us at the following address and indicate which title you would be interested in receiving (see the list at the end of guide).

Ulysses Travel Publications
4176 Rue Saint-Denis
Montréal, Québec
Canada H2W 2M5
www.ulysse.ca
e-mail: guiduly@ulysse.ca

Canadian Cataloguing in Publication Data
Rigole, Marc, 1956-
    Acapulco
    (Ulysses due south guides)
    Translation of: Acapulco
    ISBN 2-89464-062-5
1. Acapulco (Mexico) - Guidebooks. II. Title. III. Series.
F1391.A32R5313 1997   917.2'7304836   C97-940916-0

TABLE OF SYMBOLS

☎	Telephone number
⇆	Fax number
≡	Air conditioning
⊗	Ceiling fan
≈	Pool
ℜ	Restaurant
⊛	Whirlpool
ℝ	Refrigerator
K	Kitchenette
△	Sauna
⊘	Exercise room
tv	Colour television
pb	Private bathroom
sb	Shared bathroom
½b	half-board (lodging + 2 meals)
bkfst	Breakfast

ATTRACTION CLASSIFICATION

★	Interesting
★★	Worth a visit
★★★	Not to be missed

HOTEL CLASSIFICATION

$	200 pesos or less
$$	200 to 400 pesos
$$$	400 to 800 pesos
$$$$	800 to 1500 pesos
$$$$$	1500 pesos or more

Unless otherwise indicated, the prices in the guide
are for one room, double occupancy, in the high season.

RESTAURANT CLASSIFICATION

$	80 pesos or less
$$	80 to 120 pesos
$$$	120 to 200 pesos
$$$$	200 to 300 pesos
$$$$$	300 pesos or more

Unless otherwise indicated, the prices in the guide are for a meal
for one person, including taxes, but not drinks and tip.

All prices in this guide are in pesos.

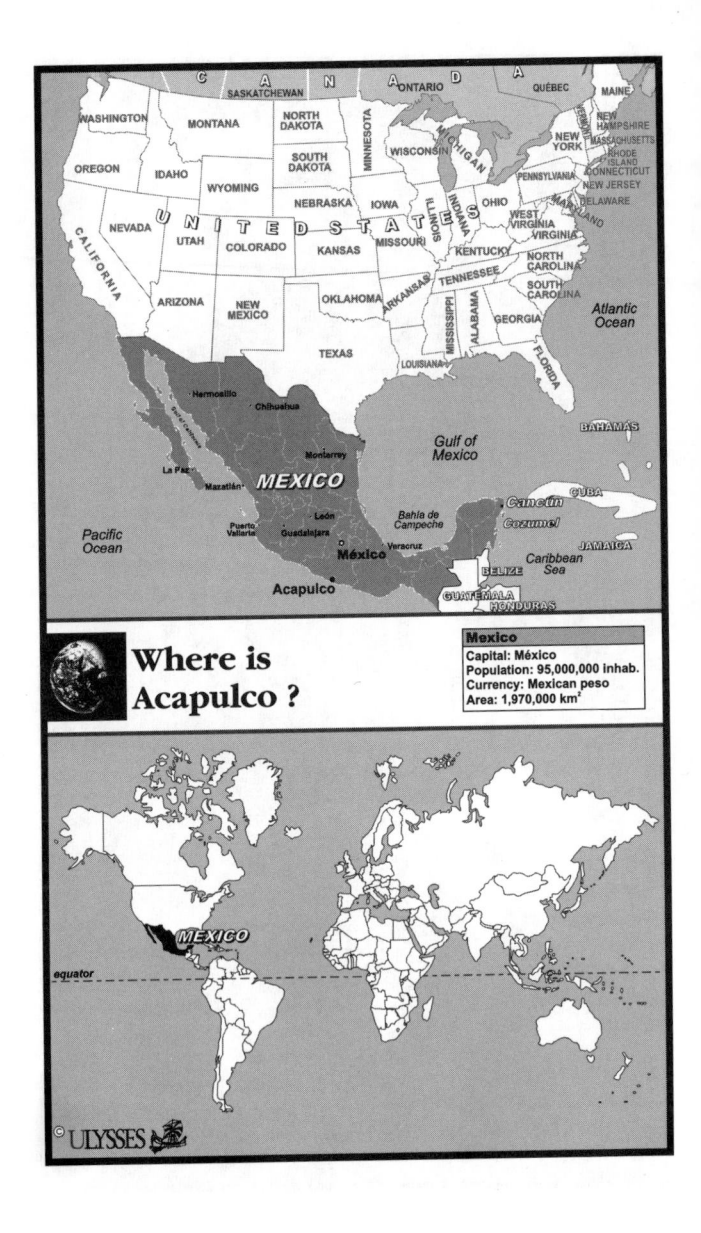

Where is Acapulco ?

Mexico
Capital: México
Population: 95,000,000 inhab.
Currency: Mexican peso
Area: 1,970,000 km²

© ULYSSES

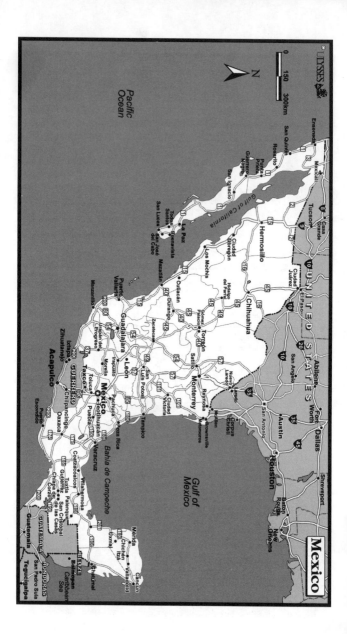

T he splendid Bay of Acapulco (Bahía de Acapulco), in the State of Guerrero, on the Pacific coast, is a choice destination. Inhabited by nearly 1.5 million people, Acapulco lives up to its reputation as a city that never sleeps. This chapter will help visitors familiarize themselves with the customs of the fabulous country that is Mexico.

GEOGRAPHY

Mexico covers a total area of 1,972,545 square kilometres. The State of Guerrero, where Acapulco and Taxco are located, is one of 31 states. Its capital is Chipalcinango, a city with few attractions located midway between Acapulco and Taxco. The State of Guerrero is particularly mountainous and constitutes a substantial barrier between the Pacific coast and the *altiplano* where the country's capital, México D.F. (Mexico City), is located. The state was named after Vicente Guerrero, who fought in the Mexican War of Independence.

Situated at 100° longitude west (opposite Texas and Manitoba) and at 17° latitude north, Acapulco boasts an enviable location that enables residents to enjoy a warm climate year round.

FAUNA

Unfortunately, travellers will have few opportunities to see tropical fauna in Acapulco. They'll be lucky to spot a few urbanized lizards or maybe an iguana that has lost its way. And yet, Mexico, like neighbouring Central America, is home to an extremely wide variety of animals.

FLORA

Thanks to its climate, the Acapulco region is overrun with tropical vegetation, which thrives in spite of the unbridled urbanization. Of course, you'll get to enjoy this luxuriance at the dining table as well, as you can feast not only on cactus (*nopal*) and avocado, but also on guavas, papayas, mangoes and even cacao, which is used to make an extremely unusual, spicy sauce (*mole poblano* or *mole oaxaqueña*) for chicken. Chocolate chicken? Why not!

THE POPULATION

Mexico has over 95 million inhabitants. The population has increased sharply since 1960, when it totalled 60 million. However, the growth rate, 3.2% in peak years, is continually declining and now stands at about 1.9% annually. As a result of the population explosion of the last 35 years, however, more young people than the economy can easily absorb are still coming onto the job market.

In this context, the U.S.-Mexican border is of central importance. Stretching over 3,000 kilometres, it is the longest boundary in the world separating a rich nation from a developing one. Millions of Mexicans already live in the United States, and hundreds of thousands move there, legally and illegally, each year. One of the undeclared goals of the North American Free Trade Agreement (NAFTA), signed by the United States, Canada and Mexico, was to check this flood of immigrants, as the U.S. government would prefer to link the Mexican and American economies rather than invest massive amounts in closing the border. For the same reason—to prevent a massive

influx of immigrants and stabilize the economy of this major client and supplier—the United States played an important role in helping Mexico overcome the economic crisis of 1995, lending the country 40 billion dollars.

The population of Acapulco, for its part, is 1.5 million, making the city a metropolis as well as a very popular seaside resort.

A BRIEF HISTORY

It is now believed that people began crossing the Bering Strait, which separates Asia from Alaska, 50,000 years ago, and thus started populating the American continent, which theretofore had no human inhabitants. How fast they moved southward remains a mystery, but archaeological evidence indicates that there were human beings in Mexico 29,000 years ago. Later, with the development of agriculture, which produced extra food, a portion of the population was able to focus on scientific and technological research. Thus emerged the first Meso-American civilization, that of the Olmecs, which flourished between 1000 and 350 B.C. and lived mainly on the east coast of Mexico. Later civilizations left behind impressive temples, dramatic sculptures and other traces of their societies. Among these are the Zapotecs, the Mixtecs, the Toltecs and the famous Mayas, who ruled over the Yucatán and Guatemala. It is known that the Mayas succeeded in creating a very precise calendar and that their monuments feature precise astrogeodesic references, but that they also carried out human sacrifices to placate the gods. This civilization fell into a rapid decline around A.D. 900, probably as a result of several consecutive years of drought. When the Spanish arrived, it was the Aztecs who were in control, with Tenochtitlán (present-day Mexico City) as their capital.

The tale of the Spaniards' encounter with the Aztecs has given rise to all sorts of speculation, but one thing is certain: it was one of the most important and troubling moments in the history of the world. The first contact between the Mexicans and the Spanish took place in 1512, when the priest Jerónimo de Aguilar and the navigator Gonzalo Guerrero were taken prisoner by the Mayas on the shores of the Yucatán. Guerrero won the respect of his captors, learned their language and married Princess Zacil. The couple had three sons, who were the first

mestizos. In 1519, the zealous conquistador Hernan Cortés set out from Cuba without authorization with a fleet of about 10 boats and 500 men, freed Aguilar, who was still being held captive on the island of Cozumel, and made him his interpreter. Cortés then headed into the centre of the future Mexico. Near present-day Veracruz, he met with the emissaries of Aztec chief Montezuma. The chief believed Cortés and his companions to be messengers of the god Quetzalcóatl; the Aztec religion predicted the arrival of a god, who would come from the east, around 1519. The red carpet was thus rolled out for the Spanish in the great city of Tenochtitlán, which was at least as big as, if not bigger than, the largest European cities at the time. They stayed there undisturbed for several months.

Nevertheless, the Europeans felt themselves to be prisoners, and perhaps they truly were. A number of Aztec leaders were supposedly plotting an attack, and Cortés, deciding to take the initiative, captured Montezuma and held him hostage. The chief, still thinking that Cortés might be a god, tried to make his people believe he was still free in order to prevent an attack on the Spanish. The Spaniards, meanwhile, began their programme of destruction, starting with the Aztec idols.

During this period, the Spanish Crown sent an expedition to stop Cortés. Upon learning this, Cortés hastened to Veracruz with some of his men. He defeated the army sent to stop him and returned to Tenochtitlán, where fighting had broken out. He was allowed entry into the city, but only so that it would be easier to surround him. Montezuma, still alive, tried to defuse the situation. He died on the battlefield; some people claim he was killed by the Spanish, others by his own people.

On June 30, 1520, the so-called Noche Triste (Sad Night), the Spanish were defeated and left the city. They did not give up the fight, however. Since arriving in Mexico, they had managed to ally themselves with the various tribes hostile to the Aztecs. With this invaluable support, they patiently constructed boats in pieces, which they then transported beyond the mountains, assembled and put in the lake surrounding the capital. On August 13, 1521, after three months of bitter fighting, the Spaniards and their native allies seized Tenochtitlán, which had already been destroyed in the battle.

In 1522, Cortés had the city rebuilt. It was thenceforth named Mexico City and became the capital of Mexico.

The Spanish established the *encomienda* system, under which soldiers were granted pieces of property and control over the natives living there, who had to farm the land; in return, the soldiers were expected to convert the natives to Christianity and "civilize" them. In the Acapulco region, the Yopes constantly rebelled against the Spanish, and in 1523 Gonzalo de Sandoval was sent here to pacify them.

After centuries of oppression, the populace finally revolted in 1810. Natives, mestizos and Creoles (Spaniards born in Mexico) all took part in the rebellion. The insurgents won independence, but did not attain the peace and prosperity they had hoped for. In 1846, a war broke out between Mexico and the United States. For the sum of 15 million dollars, the Americans acquired modern-day Texas, New Mexico, Arizona and California. Mexico thus lost everything north of the Río Bravo (Rio Grande) — half its territory at the time.

Benito Juárez García, the first aboriginal president of Mexico, took office in 1858. He instituted an education programme and set up a rail network. However, the country went bankrupt, forcing him to suspend payment of its debt, and France seized the opportunity to intervene in Mexico's affairs. Napoleon III installed Emperor Maximilian of Austria and his wife Charlotte of Saxe-Cobourg-Gotha at the head of the country, which they ruled for three years. Nevertheless, in 1867, Juárez managed to return to power and had the emperor shot.

Next came Porfirio Díaz, one of Juárez's generals, who ruled as a dictator for 35 years. Deprived of such basic civil liberties as freedom of the press, Mexico nevertheless experienced a period of peace and economic development until a revolution aiming to put an end to the dictatorship broke out in 1910. Over a million people died during this period, which still haunts the Mexican collective imagination. Two legendary heroes emerged during this revolution: Pancho Villa, an anarchist looking for personal power, and Emilio Zapata, who was fighting for agrarian reform and the abolition of discriminatory practices. Today, the native movement in Chiapas claims the latter as its spiritual leader, its members declaring themselves "Zapatistas". The revolution ended in 1917, and Madero was brought to

power. He gradually reestablished civil liberties, but was overthrown and executed. During this tumultuous period, the country's leaders were assassinated one by one. In 1927, the *Partido Revolucionnario Institucional* (PRI) was founded; it took power and quickly instituted agrarian reforms. In 1934, it nationalized the oil industry. The party has been ruling the country continuously since then.

A Brief History of Acapulco

It was in 1532, while exploring the Pacific coast, that the Spanish conquistadors discovered the Bay of Acapulco and named it Puerto Marqués. At first, the modest port of Puerto Marqués served as a jumping-off point for the exploration of the California coast and a secondary base for Pizarro and his troops, who were busy colonizing Peru at the time. However, the main reasons behind Puerto Marqués's growth were the discovery of new shipping routes to Asia and more particularly the development of trade with the Philippines. In the early 17th century, the Spanish built an imposing fort, Fuerte San Diego, to protect the bay from pirate attacks. Thanks to this fort, ships owned by the Spanish Crown were able to stop here and safely unload precious merchandise from Asia, a practice that continued until the end of the 18th century. These goods were then transported by land to Puerto Veracruz and loaded onto other ships headed for the mother country. After the colonial era, however, the little port fell into oblivion and stagnation, and it wasn't until the dawn of the 20th century that the Bay of Acapulco began to attract attention again. The beauty of the setting, combined with its ideal location, not too far from Mexico City, were at the root of this renaissance. Eager to escape the stress of life in the capital, the country's elite gradually invaded the area, and the bay slowly metamorphosed into a first-rate seaside resort. In 1927, the construction of a direct road link between the capital of the State of Guerrero and Mexico City confirmed the bay's new status and accelerated its development. Finally, the last step in Acapulco's rise to fame occurred between the 1930s and the 1960s, when an impressive number of notables of all different manner (stars, presidents, writers, millionaires, etc.) flocked to the area and succumbed to its charm. The "pearl of the Pacific", as it was dubbed by the media, became known around the world as an earthly paradise. Although new Edens have since emerged all

over the country, Acapulco is still a name that triggers the fantasies of many pleasure-seekers with a taste for the exotic. About four million people—half of them from abroad—visit the "belle of the Pacific" each year.

POLITICS

On paper, Mexico is a democracy, but in reality the vast majority of its citizens do not feel in control of their destiny and their government. When the revolution began in 1929, the Institutional Revolutionary Party (PRI) took power and has kept it ever since, thus creating a party dictatorship, to the such an extent that the recent upheavals in Mexican history, such as the 1995 assassination of the PRI's presidential candidate, Luis Donaldo Colosio, and that of the party's secretary general, Francisco Ruíz Massieu, several months later, are more the result of fighting amongst the various factions of the PRI than amongst the different political parties. However, the other parties are gaining ground, especially the Democratic Revolution Party (PRD), which backs Cuauhtémoc Cárdenas, the new mayor of Mexico City and their most likely candidate for the presidential election in the year 2000. The other opposition party, the National Action Party (PAN), is so tightly controlled by the Catholic church that its leaders are trying to close the gay bars in Guadalajara, the country's second largest city. During the July 1997 elections, the PRI only obtained 38.7% of the vote, while the PAN obtained 27% and the PRD 25.6% (up from 16.6% in 1994). Mexicans can thus look forward to a democratization of the political system and a major crackdown on corruption. The scrutiny of the international press, fixed on Mexico for several years now, could play a significant role in bringing these changes about.

It was in the State of Guerrero, where Acapulco is located, that the army assassinated 17 peasants on June 28, 1995, leading to the resignation of the governor, who was trying to cover up the soldiers' role in this grim episode of the peasantry's struggle against the government. A silent revolt is brewing among both the peasants and the natives two underprivileged segments of Mexican society who have lost all confidence in the political system and unfortunately feel driven to resort to violence in order to change things. The events of 1994, in the State of Chiapas, did, however, succeed in forcing the political

community to modify its practices considerably and there is hope that a truly democratic system will take root in Mexico over the next few years.

THE ECONOMY

In the 1970s, the Mexican economy underwent significant growth, thanks to the discovery of more petroleum deposits and the explosive increase in the price of oil implemented by the Organization of Petroleum Exporting Countries (OPEC). Mexico's oil reserves were estimated to be 60 billion barrels. However, the beginning of the 1980s brought disillusionment. The price of oil dropped, and as a result it was no longer financially viable to exploit some of the country's oil deposits. Petroleum exports no longer brought in the same profits, and Mexico, which had not managed to diversify its economy, experienced a serious crisis. As it always had in the past, the tourist industry, bolstered by a weak peso which attracted a greater number of visitors and thus an injection of foreign currency, helped keep the country afloat. The manufacturing industry also did its share to help. It is made up chiefly of subcontractors who do business with big American companies. When the peso is low, it is to these companies' advantage to have their goods produced in Mexico; inefficient as this production might often be, the wages are low.

Unfortunately, the 1980s were not marked by a decrease in protectionism in Mexico, as they were elsewhere in the world, but rather an increase, one example being the nationalization of the banks. The country thus became bogged down by often inefficient methods of production (rather than developing modern, efficient cars, the VW bug is still made here, its domestic sales bolstered by the formidable barriers facing automobile imports); computers, which the country needed desperately in order to bring itself up to date, were imported and thus exorbitantly taxed, with the result that they were in very limited use here. The government subsidized crops that yielded little, thus using up manpower that could be put to better use elsewhere. Cut off from major international trends in technological modernization, Mexico could only slip backwards, especially with the declining value of primary resources on world markets. It was not enough for Mexico to be the world's largest producer of silver; the global economy had metamor-

phosed, and was now based on added value, expertise, creativity and information.

It was in this context that Carlos Salinas de Gortari negotiated the free trade agreement, turning his back on years of protectionism. Mexico thus woke up one day to find itself in the centre of an open North American market, a situation it was not prepared for. In accordance with the free trade agreement, subsidies to inefficient farms were cut, putting hundreds of thousands of workers out of a job, though no measures had been instituted to ease the transition. Mexicans instantly had access to thousands of less expensive American products, which had theretofore been heavily taxed. They thus started buying massive quantities of imported goods. During this period, the country's strengths were not taken advantage of quickly enough, and years of protectionism caused Mexicans to lose sight of what these advantages actually were. The inevitable occurred: the trade balance was abruptly skewed, the peso took a drastic plunge and the government was unable to pay its creditors.

It was not free trade that was to blame for this crisis, but rather the country's lack of preparation to make the transition from extreme protectionism to full participation in the global economy.

As mentioned above, one of the reasons the United States decided to sign the free trade agreement was to check the flood of immigrants coming over the border. We should also add that the increase in American exports is much greater to developing countries, like Mexico, and that in order for this growth to continue, these countries' economies have to be stable. This also explains why the Americans lent Mexico 40 billion dollars in 1995.

Of course, for the tourist industry, the crisis of 1995 led to another period of dramatic growth, as North Americans and Europeans alike seized the opportunity for inexpensive vacations in the sun. In late 1995, Mexico was one of the best bargains on the planet for sun-worshippers.

Throughout 1996, inflation, hovering at around 20%, would change this situation a bit, but Mexico is still a very good value for travellers. As far as jobs are concerned, the picture has

gradually brightened. Little by little, Mexico has increased its exports; for example, many more furnishings and decorative objects from Mexico are now available on the North American market. Outlets have been found for Mexican produce all over North America and even in Europe. Industrial complexes have been established in northern Mexico to satisfy the demands of the flourishing market in the southern United States.

MUSIC

Despite the presence of the American giant north of the border, which controls the distribution of records and inundates the country with its television programmes, Mexico holds its own and continues to favour Latin American music. It is even producing its own stars and exporting them to the United States. This is a truly remarkable phenomenon, a testimony to the extraordinary vitality of Latin American culture. Despite the obvious Americanization of Mexican society, less American music is played on the radio in Mexico than in Canada or Germany!

Mexico has its trendy stars, like Monica Narango or Ana Gabriel, but still loves such celebrities of the past as Chelo Silva or Javier Solis. Furthermore, unlike in the U.S. and Canada, hits of the sixties and seventies still get air play in Mexico. The retro trend has apparently always been popular here. Perhaps this indicates a greater attachment to the past than in the societies to the north.

We recommend that you to dive headlong into Latin American culture and stock up on records that are likely to be hard to find in your country. This will enable you to recreate a holiday atmosphere back home and improve your knowledge of Spanish. Ediciones Pentagrama puts out albums by a number of socially involved artists and singers who strive to keep regional folk traditions alive.

Among the Mexican singers that you'll hear frequently during your stay here, and whose albums are readily available in stores, the following occupy a truly special place in the pantheon of Mexican music:

Oscar Chávez: This socially involved artist, who has been making music for 40 years now, is always ready to defend a cause and denounce corruption. His songs, whose music is steeped in Mexican tradition, are often veritable political caricatures.

Selena: Born in Texas or Mexican parents, Selena managed to build a career for herself in the United States, where she became the idol of the Latin American community before being murdered a few years ago. Her brothers and sisters made up part of her band and wrote some of her songs. Her tragic end made her a legendary figure, and it is doubtful that we have heard all we're going to hear about her. Her life story has already been told in books and a movie.

Juan Gabriel: This very popular singer has experimented with all different styles, from rock to *mariachi*. He is an undeniably gifted songwriter, creating new songs that blend in perfectly with the Mexican folk heritage.

Linda Ronstadt: Born of a Mexican father but raised in Texas, Linda Ronstadt contributed to the rebirth of Mexican folk music among an American audience that still feels closely linked to Mexican culture. She has recorded two albums in Spanish that highlight the *ranchera* style.

Chelo Silva: Chelo Silva, who first became a star in the 1950s, sings about Mexico in evocative songs full of cheeky humour.

Grupo i: In the discotheques listed in this guide, you'll often hear song sequences, unless you're lucky enough to be somewhere where there's live music, like the Tropicana (see p 101). The fad for these tropical bands (*banda musica*) took off in the early 1980s, and they still appeal to night owls. Grupo i is one of the favourites. They have recorded nine records so far in the Tropi-rollo series, featuring tropical "rolls" of eight or nine songs end to end.

Vicky Carr: You might "discover" Vicky Carr by chance during a transvestite show. Along with Chelo Silva, this 1960s singer/songwriter is one of the most frequently imitated celebrities (you might also spot Céline Dion or Dolly Parton!). Her album *Recuerdo a Javier Solis* is a collection of her best songs, which she sings magnificently in her deep, rich voice.

Monica Naranjo, **Ana Gabriel**, **Yuri**, **Shakira** and **Laura Leon** are among the other singers you'll hear frequently.

The following is a list of some of the styles of music you'll encounter in Mexico:

Ranchera: Distinguished by its passionate cries, its *aïe, aïe, aïe*s, its melancholy mood and its fatalism, *ranchera* is probably the style that people associate most closely with traditional Mexican music.

Cumbia mexicana: Originally Columbian, *cumbia*, with its fiery, syncopated rhythms, is probably the style most typical of Latin American music.

Norteño: This style from the northern part of the country is characterized by nasal singing and the use of the accordion.

Mariachi: Native to the State of Jalisco, where Puerto Vallarta is located, Mariachi bands have evolved into groups of six to 10 musicians playing the violin, the guitar and the trumpet. They are generally paid by the song.

Banda: This brass-oriented style, which has developed over the past 10 years, borrows from *norteño* and *cumbia*.

LITERATURE

Typically Latin American, Mexican literature is both surrealistic and down to earth. The following are a few authors whose works you can enjoy in their English translation:

Octavio Paz: The winner of the 1990 Nobel Prize for Literature, Paz may be considered the most important Mexican author of the 20th century. Particularly noteworthy among his works of poetry, through which he is always fighting for noble values and against the pressure of contemporary politics, is *El laberinto de la soledad* (1950, *The Labyrinth of Solitude*), a sort of psychoanalytical study of the Mexican character that explores love, death, American-Mexican relations and machismo all at once. The Mexican ambassador to India, he has written a number of works analyzing the similarities and differences between the east and the west, between India and

Mexico, one example being *Conjunciones y disjunciones* (1969).

Carlos Fuentes: The Mexican ambassador to Paris from 1975 to 1978, Carlos Fuentes is probably the most cosmopolitan of all Mexican authors. His entire body of work is devoted to the search for the true Mexican identity by means of a "Balzac-style" description of society. In *Cristóbal nonato*, one of his recent works, the leading character is born on the Acapulco beach in 1999.

Alberto Ruy Sánchez: Born in 1951, Alberto Ruy Sánchez is not only a writer but also the managing editor of Artes de Mexico, which puts out beautiful books on Mexico, as well as a literary magazine. This prolific author's work features a skilful blend of poetry and action.

PAINTING AND CERAMICS

During your stay in Acapulco, you might have a chance to admire the paintings of Cristina Rubalcava. A number of her works adorn the rooms of the Hotel Elcano (see p 76). All tinged with poetry and humanism, her canvasses depict Mexican legends and focus on the Mexican people.

Cristina Rubalcava

Born in Mexico City in 1943, painter Cristina Rubalcava lived and worked in Paris in the 1970s. After her work was featured in various exhibitions around the world, the Elcano hotel commissioned her to execute a series of paintings and lithographs to lend character to the premises. Drawing inspiration from the 1950s and using a style similar to naive art, she created a cheerful blend of images typical of the Bay of Acapulco. For example, one painting shows countless palm trees; dance floors set up right on the beach; bands; a Virgin of Guadalupe and some *clavadistas* making their dangerous leaps, all set against an ocean backdrop teeming with exuberant marine life. As if to lend a beat to this dynamic scene, Rubalcava even threw in snippets of popular songs here and there.

You might also discover the work of ceramist Emilia Castillo, either in her shop in Taxco (see p 142) or in Acapulco, at the Madeiras restaurant (see p 115).

PRACTICAL INFORMATION

This section is intended to help you plan your trip to Acapulco. It also includes general information and practical advice designed to familiarize you with local customs.

ENTRANCE FORMALITIES

Passport

To enter Mexico, you must have a valid passport. This is by far the most widely accepted piece of identification, and therefore the safest. As a general rule, the expiration date should not fall less than three months after your date of arrival. If you have a return ticket, however, your passport need only be valid for the duration of your stay. If not, proof of sufficient funds may be required. For travellers from most Western countries (Canada, United States, Australia, New Zealand, Western European countries) a simple passport is enough, no visa is necessary. Other citizens are advised to contact the nearest consulate to see if they need a visa to enter. Since requirements for entering the country can change quickly, it is wise to double-check them before leaving.

Travellers are advised to keep a photocopy of the most important pages of their passport, as well as to write down its number and date of issue. If ever this document is lost or stolen, this will facilitate the replacement process. In case of such an event, contact your country's embassy or consulate (see addresses below) in order to be reissued an equivalent document as soon as possible.

Minors Entering the Country

In Mexico, all individuals under 18 years of age are legally considered minors. Each traveller under the age of 18 is therefore required to present written proof of his or her status upon entering the country, namely, a letter of consent signed by his or her parents or legal guardians and notarized or certified by a representative of the court (a justice of the peace or a commissioner for oaths).

A minor accompanied by only one parent must carry a signed letter of consent from the other parent, which also must be notarized or certified by a representative of the court.

If the minor has only one legally recognized parent, he or she must have a paper attesting to that fact. Again, this document must be notarized or certified by a justice of the peace of a commissioner for oaths.

Airline companies require adults who are meeting minors unaccompanied by their parents or an official guardian to provide their address and telephone number.

Customs Declaration Forms and Tourist Cards

On the way to Mexico, the flight attendants will hand out a questionnaire to all air passengers; this is a customs declaration form, which must be completed before your arrival.

Upon your arrival in Mexico, after your proof of citizenship and customs declaration form have been checked, the customs officer will give you a blue tourist card. This card is free and authorizes its holder to visit the country. Do not to lose it, as

you must return it to Mexican immigration when you leave the country. Take the same precautions as you did with your passport, by recording the tourist card number somewhere else — on your airline ticket, for example.

Airport Departure Tax

Except for children under two years of age, all passengers taking international flights out of Mexico are required to pay a tax of about $13.37 US. The major airlines often include this tax in the ticket price; ask your travel agent.

Customs

Travellers are allowed to bring in three litres of wine or spirits, 400 cigarettes and a reasonable amount of perfume or eau de toilette for personal use. Of course, it is strictly forbidden to bring any drugs or firearms into the country. All personal medication, especially psychotropic drugs, must have a prescription label on them.

EMBASSIES AND CONSULATES

Foreign Embassies and Consulates in Mexico

Embassies and consulates can provide precious information to visitors who find themselves in a difficult situation (for example, loss of passport or in the event of an accident or death, they can provide names of doctors, lawyers, etc.). They deal only with urgent cases, however. It should be noted that costs arising from such services are not paid by these consular missions. Here are a few addresses of consulates and embassies in the federal capital Mexico City and in Acapulco. Taxco possesses neither an embassy nor a consulate.

Australia
Embassy: Ruben Darío 55, Col. Polanco, 11560 - Mexico D.F., ☎ (5) 531-5225, ≈ (5) 203-8431.

Belgium
Embassy: Avenida Alfredo de Musset, n° 41, Colonia Polanco, 11550 - Mexico, D.F., ☎ (5) 280-0758, ⇌ (5) 280-0208.

Canada
Embassy: Calle Schiller, n° 529, (Rincón del Bosque), Colonia Polanco, 11560 - Mexico, D.F., ☎ (5) 254-3288 or toll-free 91-800-70-629, ⇌ (5) 254-8554.
Consulate: Plaza Marbella (near the restaurant La Petite Belgique), ☎ 84-13-05, ⇌ 84-13-06

Germany
Consulate: Antón de Alaminos, n° 46, Fracc. Costa Azul, ☎ 84-74-37, ⇌ 84-38-10.

Great Britain
Embassy: Lerma 71, Col. Cuauhtémoc, 06500 Mexico D.F., ☎ (525) 207-2089, ⇌ (525) 207-7672.
Consulate: Hotel Las Brisas, ☎ 84-66-05, 84-16-50 or 84-22-69, ⇌ 81-21-58.

Holland
Consulate: Hotel El Presidente, C. Del Ciruelo, n° 13, D-4, Fracc. Hornos Insurgentes, ☎ 84-17-00, ext. 17.

Italy
Embassy: Avenida Paseo de las Palmas, n° 1994, 11000 - Mexico, D.F., ☎ (5) 596-3655, ⇌ (5) 596-7710
Consulate: Av. Gran Vía Tropical, n° 615-B, ☎ 83-38-75 or 82-48-55, ⇌ 81-25-33.

New Zealand
Embassy: Jose Luis Lagrange 103, 10th floor, Colonia Los Morales, Polanco, 11510 Mexico D.F., ☎ (5) 281-5486, ⇌ (5) 281-5212.

Norway
Consulate: C. Juan de Dios Bonilla, n° 27, Facc. Costa Azul, ☎ 84-35-25, ⇌ 84-35-25.

Spain
Embassy: Galileo, n° 114, Colonia Polanco, 11560 - Mexico, D.F., ☎ (5) 596-3655, ⇌ (5) 596-7710.

Consulate: Av. Cuauhtémoc y Universidad, n° 2, ☎ 86-72-05, 86-24-91 or 86-24-66, ✆ 84-48-56.

Switzerland
Embassy: Torre Optima, 11. Stock, Avenida Paseo de las Palmas, n° 405, Lomas de Chapltepec, 11000 - Mexico, D.F., ☎ (5) 520-8535 or (5) 520-3003, ✆ (5) 520-8685.
Consulate: Av. Insurgentes, n° 2-4, Fracc. Hornos Insurgentes, ☎ 85-29-35, ✆ 85-29-36.

United States
Embassy: Passeo de la Reforma, n° 1305, 06500 - Mexico, D.F., ☎ (5) 211-0042 or 208-3373, ✆ (5) 511-9980.
Consulate: Hotel Club del Sol, Mezzanine-office, n° 8, ☎ 85-72-07, ✆ 83-19-69.

Mexican Embassies and Consulates Abroad

In Australia
Mexican Embassy: 49 Bay Street, Double Bay, Sydney, NSW, 2028, ☎ (02) 326-1292.

In Belgium
Mexican Embassy: 164, chaussée de la Hulpe, 1st floor, 1170 - Bruxelles, ☎ (32-2) 676-0711, ✆ (32-2) 676-9312.

In Canada
Mexican Embassy: 45 O'Connor Street, Office 1500, Ottawa, Ontario, K1P 1A4, ☎ (613) 233-8988 or 233-9572, ✆ (613) 235-9123.
Consulate General of Mexico: 2000, rue Mansfield, Bureau 1015, 10th floor, Montréal, Québec, H3A 2Z7, ☎ (514) 288-2502, ✆ (514) 288-8287.
Consulate General of Mexico: Commerce Court West, 99 Bay Street, Toronto, Ontario, M5L 1E9, ☎ (416) 368-2875, ✆ (416) 368-3478.

In Germany
Mexican Embassy: Adenaueralle 100, 53113 Bonn, ☎ (228) 91-48-60.

In Great Britain
Mexican Embassy: 8 Halkin Street, London SWIX 8QR, ☎ (0171) 235-6393.

In Italy
Mexican Embassy: Via Lazzaro Spallanzani 16, 00161 Rome, ☎ (396) 440-4400.

In New Zealand
Mexican Embassy: 111-115 Customhouse Quay, 8th floor, Wellington, ☎ (644) 472-5555.

In Spain
Mexican Embassy: Carrera de San Geronimo, 46, 28014 Madrid, ☎ (341) 369-2814.

In Switzerland
Mexican Embassy: Bernstrasse, n° 57, 3005 - Berne, ☎ (031) 351-1875, ⇆ (031) 351-3492.
Note: there are honorary consulates of Mexico in Zurich and Lausanne; their addresses are available from the embassy in Berne.

In the United States
Mexican Embassy: 1911 Pennsylvania Avenue, N.W., 20006 - Washington D.C., ☎ (202) 728-1633, ⇆ (202) 728-1698.
Mexican Consulate: 8 East 41st Street, New York, N.Y., 10017, ☎ (212) 689-0456.
Mexican Consulate: 2401 W. 6th St., Los Angeles, CA, 90057 ☎ (213) 351-6800.
Mexican Consulate: 300 North Michigan Ave., 2nd floor, Chicago, IL, 60601, ☎ (312) 855-0056.

  TOURIST INFORMATION

Mexican Tourist Associations Abroad

In North America
Mexico Hotline: ☎ 1-800-44-MEXICO or 1-800-446-3942.

In Canada
1, Place Ville-Marie, Bureau 1526, Montréal, Québec, H3B 3M9, ☎ (514) 871-1052, ⊷ (514) 871-3825.
2 Bloor Street West, Office 1801, Toronto, Ontario, M4W 3E2, ☎ (416) 925-0704, 925-2753 or 925-1876, ⊷ (416) 925-6061.

In Germany
Wiesenhüttenplatz 26, d-60329 Frankfurt am Main 1 Germany, ☎ (4969) 25-3413.

In Great Britain
60-61 Trafalgar Sq., London WC2 N5DS, United Kingdom, ☎ 44 173-1058.

In Italy
Via Barberini, n° 23, 00187 - Rome, ☎ (39-6) 25-3413 or 25-3541, ⊷ (39-6) 25-3755.

In Spain
Calle Velázquez, n° 126, 28006 - Madrid, ☎ (34-1) 261-3520 or 261-1827, ⊷ (34-1) 411-0759.

In the United States
405 Park Ave., Suite 1401, New York, N.Y., 10022, ☎ (212) 755-7261.
10100 Santa Monica Blvd., Suite 224, Los Angeles CA, 90067, ☎ (310) 203-8191.
70 E. Lake St., Suite 1413, Chicago, IL, 60601, ☎ (312) 565-2778.

ENTERING THE COUNTRY

By Airplane

From Canada

During the winter, many airlines organize non-stop charter flights to Acapulco from most major Canadian cities. Canadian travellers can also travel through an American gateway city (see below).

Air Transat, Canada 3000 and Royal all offer direct charter flights during the winter from Montreal, Toronto and Vancouver. Canadian Airlines (☎ *1-800-387-3401)* flies to Mexico City, where travellers can take one of many domestic flights linking Acapulco and the capital. Air Canada and Continental jointly offer a route to Acapulco through Houston. These regular flights are more comfortable, more flexible and offer the possibility of accumulating air miles. Mexicana is planning to institute a regular Montreal-Mexico City route with the option of continuing on to Acapulco.

From the United States

There are a multitude of daily flights between Mexico and the United States. American Airlines, Aeromexico, Mexicana and many other airlines fly directly to Acapulco, either non-stop, or with a stop-over in Mexico City. During the winter it is possible to find tickets at particularly inexpensive rates.

From Europe

Depending on the season and the availability of flights, it can prove more economical for Europeans to travel to the United States (Houston, Miami or New York) and from there take a charter flight to Acapulco.

KLM and British Airways have flights to Mexico City from Amsterdam and London, respectively. Once in the capital connector flights are plentiful.

Airport

The **Juan N. Alvarez International Airport** is situated 23 kilometres from downtown, on a narrow strip of land between the ocean and immense Tres Palos lagoon. The airport is divided into two sections, one for international flights and the other, spread over two floors, for domestic flights. On the ground floor of the latter are the airline counters and car rental counters, an exchange bureau, postal services, public telephones and two automatic teller machines (Visa, MasterCard

and Cirrus Plus are accepted). On the second floor are a few shops, newsstands, a restaurant and two snack bars.

As in all of Mexico's international airports, travellers going through customs are asked to press a button which activates a green light, which means that they can enter the country with no further ado, or a red light, which means that they will have to be searched first.

If your stomach is growling before your departure, the small snack bar, **Snack Aca**, on the second floor of the domestic terminal, is less expensive than the airport restaurant, and you will be able to have one last *comida corrida* for the modest sum of 28 pesos.

For last-minute gift shopping, **Mussfeldt Design**, on the second floor of the domestic terminal offers a good selection of brightly coloured t-shirts. Since this is the airport, expect to pay the tidy sum of 95 pesos per shirt. The duty-free stores are located on the ground floor, past the customs check of course.

To reach the airport from downtown, and vice-versa, see p 54.

HEALTH

Mexico is a wonderful country to visit. Unfortunately, travellers do run the risk of contracting certain diseases there, such as malaria, typhoid, diphtheria, tetanus, polio and hepatitis A and B. Though such cases are rare they do occur. When planning your trip, therefore, consult your doctor (or a clinic for travellers) about what precautions to take. Don't forget that preventing these illnesses is easier than curing them. It is therefore practical to take medications, vaccines and necessary precautions in order to avoid medical problems likely to become serious. If, however, you do have to see a doctor, most large hotels have in-house medical offices. If not, hotel staff or on-site travel agents will be able to help you find a doctor. We have listed the addresses of hospitals in the "Practical Information" section of each chapter.

Illnesses

Cases of hepatitis A and B, AIDS and certain venereal diseases have been reported in Mexico, so it is wise to take necessary precautions.

Bodies of fresh water are often contaminated with the bacteria that causes schistosomiasis. This illness results when a parasite invades the body and attacks the liver and nervous system, and it is difficult to treat. Swimming in fresh water should therefore be avoided.

Remember that excessive alcohol intake can cause dehydration and illness, especially when accompanied by lengthy exposure to the sun.

Because medical facilities are sometimes rudimentary make sure (if possible) that quality control tests have been properly carried out before any blood transfusion.

Tap water in Acapulco and Taxco is not purified. The medical problems travellers are most likely to encounter are usually a result of poorly treated water containing bacteria that cause upset stomach, diarrhea or fever. To avoid this risk drink only bottled water, which is available just about all over the country. When buying a bottle, whether in a restaurant or a store, always make sure that it is well sealed. In Acapulco only a few of the large hotels have water treatment systems; the vast majority do not and travellers are advised against drinking tap water. Fruit and vegetables rinsed in tap water (those not peeled before eating) can cause the same problems. Visitors should be doubly careful in low budget restaurants, which do not always have the equipment necessary to ensure proper hygiene. The same goes for the small street vendors as well as those on the beach (be particularly careful with brochettes and grilled fish). Finally, dairy products are perfectly safe for consumption in Acapulco and Taxco.

If you do get diarrhea, there are several methods of treating it. Try to soothe your digestive system by avoiding solids and dairy products. Drink a lot of liquids to avoid dehydration, which can be dangerous. To remedy severe dehydration, drink a solution made up of one litre (4 cups) of water, three

teaspoons of salt and one teaspoon of sugar. You can also find ready-made preparations in most pharmacies– Pedialyte, for example, which is available in several flavours: natural, cherry, strawberry or coconut (this last one is the best choice). Next, gradually start reintroducing solids into your diet by eating foods that are easy to digest. Medications like Imodium, Pepto Bismol or Lomotil can help control an upset stomach and are available in most pharmacies throughout Mexico. They can, however, cause severe constipation which can allow certain bacteria to enter the bloodstream. If your symptoms persist and are severe (high fever, violent diarrhea), you may need antibiotics, in which case it is best to consult a doctor. If possible, avoid injections preferring medication taken orally.

Food and climate can also cause various health problems. Make sure that food is fresh (especially fish and meat) and that the area in which it is prepared is clean. Proper hygiene, such as washing hands frequently, will also help keep you healthy.

Insects

The discomforts caused by insects, which are not particularly numerous in Acapulco and Taxco, are limited most of the time to a few mosquito bites. Nevertheless, to avoid being bitten, cover up well in the evening (when insects are most active), avoid perfume, wear light colours (apparently light colours repel insects) and arm yourself with a good insect repellant.

Scorpions are a real nuisance, especially during the dry season, and their bites can cause high fevers, or even prove fatal to someone in a fragile state of health. Scorpions have the annoying habit of creeping into houses and other buildings on the ground floor. It is therefore necessary to take a few precautions, especially when travelling outside Acapulco. Avoid leaving your shoes on the ground and walking barefoot. Check out all the nooks and crannies in public bathrooms, and use a flashlight so you can see clearly when you're walking after dark. If you take a nap on a hammock or on a chaise longue, make sure to shake it out well before lying down on it. When walking in the mountains or the forest wear shoes and socks to protect your feet and legs. Do not walk in tall grass along roadsides. Anyone who gets bitten by a scorpion should be

taken to a doctor or a hospital immediately. The same measures apply to snake bites.

The Sun

Despite its benefits, the sun also causes numerous problems.
Always use sunblock to protect yourself from the sun's harmful
rays. Many of the sunscreens on the market do not provide
adequate protection. Before setting off on your trip, ask your
pharmacist which ones are truly effective against the dangerous rays of the sun. For the best results, apply the cream at
least 20 minutes before going out in the sun. Overexposure to
the sun can cause sunstroke, symptoms of which include
dizziness, vomiting and fever. It is important to keep well
protected and avoid prolonged exposure, especially during the
first few days of your trip, as it takes a while to get used to the
sun's strength. Even after a few days, moderate exposure is
best. A hat and pair of sunglasses are indispensable accessories
in this part of the world.

INSURANCE

Cancellation

Cancellation insurance is usually offered by the travel agent
when you buy your airplane ticket or holiday package. It
permits reimbursement for the ticket or package in the case of
cancellation of a trip due to serious illness or death. People
with no health problems do not really need this type of
protection.

Theft

Most Canadian home insurance plans protect the insured for
theft, including incidents of theft that occur outside the
country. To submit a claim, a police report must be obtained.
Depending on your coverage, it is not always useful to take out
additional insurance. Europeans should check whether their

policies cover them when they are abroad, as this is not automatically the case.

Life

Many airlines offer life insurance included in the price of the ticket. As well, many travellers already have life insurance and therefore do not need to buy an additional policy.

Health

Health insurance is without question the most useful kind of insurance for travellers. It should be purchased before setting off on a trip. The insurance policy should be as comprehensive as possible, because health care costs add up quickly, even in Mexico. When purchasing the policy, make sure it covers medical expenses of all kinds, such as hospitalization, nursing services and doctor's fees (at fairly high rates, as these are expensive). A repatriation clause, in case necessary care cannot be administered on site, is invaluable. In addition, you may have to pay upon leaving the clinic, so you should check your policy to see what provisions it includes for such instances. During your stay in Mexico, you should always keep proof that you are insured on your person to avoid any confusion in case of an accident.

CLIMATE

In a country as mountainous as Mexico, it is self-evident that the climate will not be the same in all regions. The State of Guerrero includes several climatic zones which vary as a function of altitude and geographic location. Details for Acapulco and Taxco follow.

One of the principal factors in the success of **Acapulco** is precisely the weather: hot and humid year-round. Varying by only a few degrees, the annual average temperature is between 25° C and 35° C during the day, and 20° C to 25° C at night. The only notable weather change occurs during the rainy season (from June to September), during which there are

downpours every afternoon. Despite these showers the average annual rainfall in Acapulco is only 180 centimetres.

Situated at an altitude of 1,750 metres, **Taxco** enjoys a remarkably temperate climate comparable to that of the cities of Guadalajara or Mexico. In fact, the average temperature of this town is about 21° C. At night, the town is pleasantly cool; a light sweater may be required. The months from June through September have the highest rainfall.

PACKING

The type of clothing visitors should pack varies little from one season to the next. In general, loose, comfortable cotton clothing is most practical in Acapulco. For walking in the city, as much in Taxco as in Acapulco, it is better to wear shoes that cover the entire foot, since these provide the best protection against cuts that can become infected. In fact, what with uneven sidewalks and numerous obstacles (holes, poorly installed manhole covers, stems of metal protruding from the ground, etc.), shoes protect you from possible injury. For cool evenings, in Taxco only, a long-sleeved shirt or sweater can be useful. Remember to wear rubber sandals on the beach. During the rainy season, bring a small umbrella to keep dry during the showers. When visiting certain sights (churches for example), a skirt that hangs below the knees or a pair of pants should be worn, so don't forget to include the appropriate article of clothing in your suitcase. If you intend to go on an excursion in the mountains, take along a pair of good walking shoes. Finally, don't forget to bring a sunhat and sunglasses.

Safety and Security

Acapulco survives on tourism, so security is a constant preoccupation of local authorities. A special police force dressed in white uniforms looks out for visitors' safety. These officers speak both Spanish and English. Considering the size of Acapulco, it is a particularly safe city. Nonetheless, it is obviously appropriate to follow the normal rules for personal safety. Avoid counting money in the open, and refrain from wearing ostentatious displays of jewellery (except if you are

going out to Fantasy, see p 117). Keep electronic equipment in a nondescript bag slung across your chest. Conceal travellers' cheques, passport and some cash in a money belt that fits under your clothing; this way if your bags are ever stolen you will still have the papers and money necessary to get by. Remember, the less attention you attract, the less chance you have of being robbed.

As for Taxco, the only danger posed to travellers in this peaceful little town is personal bankruptcy caused by silverware and jewellery shopping sprees! If, by misfortune, you should be robbed, do not hesitate to contact the local police, remembering to ask for a copy of the report for insurance purposes. Police stations are listed in the "Practical Information" sections of each chapter.

TRANSPORTATION

By Car

Since the main tourist attractions of Acapulco and the city's surrounding area are close to one another, and since taxis and buses are easy and inexpensive to use, we recommend that people who are limiting their stay to this city not rent a car. The same applies to Taxco, especially given the town's near impossible parking situation and the fact that urban traffic already contributes to a pollution problem in this architectural gem.

If you still want to rent a car, be aware that the cost of rental at your destination is often substantially greater than a flight-car rental package organized by a travel agency. Most of the large car rental agencies are located along the Costera and at the airport.

Car Rental Companies

Avis: International Airport, ☎ 62-00-85 or 62-00-75.

Budget: La Costera 999-5, ☎ 81-05-92, 81-05-95 or 84-88-60.

Hertz: La Costera 1945, ☎ 85-89-47, 85-68-89 or 85-69-42.

Distances between Acapulco and other Cities of Mexico

Chilpancingo: 113 km / 70 mi
Guadalajara: 934 km / 580 mi
Manzanillo: 675 km / 419 mi
Mexico City: 388 km / 241 mi
Pie de la Cuesta: 15 km / 9 mi
Puerto Marqués: 20 km / 12 mi
Taxco: 205 km / 127 m

Taxis

Taxis are probably the most efficient and safest means of getting around. It is no trouble finding a taxi as drivers are literally looking for you. The vast majority of taxis are "beetles", which can mean an uncomfortable ride. Taxis have no meters but rather function on a fixed-fare system that sometimes, with negotiation, actually proves to be rather flexible. The "sport" of haggling over the fare should be practised before embarking in the cab. As a general rule, taxis parked in front of hotels and restaurants pay a commission to these establishments and so are a little more expensive than taxis hailed in the street. The same applies to people who take it on themselves to call a taxi for you. Unless you are travelling with luggage, a tip is not required.

Buses

Public buses, known as *camiónes* in Mexico, are numerous and go just about everywhere, offering a novel and economic means of travelling all around the area. Many bus companies operate in Mexico, and the quality of service varies enormously as a function of price. Especially for trips of great distances it is emphatically recommended to travel by first class bus. These buses are generally newer, have televisions and toilets, and sometimes even offer free coffee. For the addresses of bus stations, see p 124 and p 57.

Hitchhiking

Risky business! It is highly inadvisable to hitchhike in Mexico.

FINANCIAL SERVICES

Currency

The country's currency is the nuevo peso or peso. The peso sign is $MEX or NP$. There are 10, 20, 50, 100, 200 and 500 peso bills and 1, 5, 10, 20 and 50 peso coins, as well as 5, 10, 20 and 50 centavo pieces. Prices are often also listed in US dollars, especially in touristy areas. Be careful: there are still a few old pesos in circulation, and they are only worth 1% of the new peso. In a place like a dimly lit bar, someone might try to swindle you by slipping you your change in old pesos.

Mexican currency is subject to major fluctuations, and has been devalued numerous times in recent years. The exchange rates for various foreign currencies are listed below.

Banks

The local banks are open from 9am to 3pm, Monday to Friday. Most of them will change Canadian and US dollars; fewer will change other foreign currencies. It is generally to your advantage to travel in Mexico with US dollars, as the exchange rates are better. A number of banks have automated teller machines that accept debit and credit cards.

Exchanging Money

It is illegal and inadvisable to exchange money in the street. Given the risks (theft, counterfeit bills, etc.) and the small amount of money you stand to save, it is far better to change your money at a bank or an exchange office. For the best rate of exchange, make a cash withdrawal on your credit card; this

$1 US = $7.82 MEX	$1 MEX = $0.13 US
$1 CAN = $5.67 MEX	$1 MEX = $0.18 CAN
1 £ = $12.80 MEX	$1 MEX = 0.078 £
$1 Aust = $5.81 MEX	$1 MEX = $0.17 Aust
$1 NZ = $5.02 MEX	$1 MEX = $0.20 NZ
1000 LIT = $4.34 MEX	$1 MEX = 230 LIT
1 PTA = $0.05 MEX	$1 MEX = 19.95 PTA
1 BF = $0.21 MEX	$1 MEX = 4.87 BF
1 SF = $5.16 MEX	$1 MEX = 0.19 SF
1 fl = $3.76 MEX	$1 MEX = 0.27 fl
1 DM = $4.23MEX	$1 MEX = 0.24 DM

will save you about 2%, which is generally more than the interest you'll have to pay when you get back. For the same reason, it is best to pay for purchases with your credit card whenever possible.

Exchange offices are located just about everywhere, all along the Costera in Acapulco, and near Plaza Borda in Taxco. Although these offices accept most major currencies (American and Canadian dollars, European currencies, yen, etc.), American dollars always get a better rate. Holders of Canadian or European money will find it far more advantageous to use credit cards (see above) or to exchange their money for American currency before travelling to Mexico. Passports are required for exchange transactions. Whenever possible, avoid exchanging money in hotels as their rates are especially unfavourable.

Travellers' Cheques

It is always wise to keep most of your money in travellers' cheques, which, when in US dollars, are sometimes accepted in restaurants, hotels and shops. They are also easy to exchange in most banks and foreign exchange offices. Be sure to keep a copy of the serial numbers of the cheques in a separate place, so if ever they are lost, the company that issued them can replace them quickly and easily. Nevertheless, always keep some cash on hand.

Credit Cards

Most credit cards are accepted in a large number of businesses, although in certain cases, especially in Acapulco, only American Express is accepted. In addition to being easy to use, credit cards offer the best exchange rates, and it is therefore better to pay for as many of your purchases with them as possible. When using a credit card, you will need to present your passport and write its number on the bill.

TELECOMMUNICATIONS

Mail

It costs 2.50 pesos to send a postcard or letter to Europe, 2.10 pesos to countries in North, South and Central America.

Telephone

The area code for **Acapulco** is **74**.

The area code for **Taxco** is **762**.

Calling Mexico from Abroad

From North America: Dial 011 (for the international operator) + 52 (the country code for Mexico) + the area code + local number.

From Great Britain, New Zealand, Belgium and Switzerland: Dial 00 (for the international operator) + 52 (the country code for Mexico) + the area code + local number.

From Australia: Dial 0011 (for the international operator) + 52 (the country code for Mexico) + the area code + local number.

Calling Abroad from Mexico

As a general rule, it is more economical to call collect; the best option for Canadian, American and British citizens wishing to call someone in their native country is through a direct collect-call service (eg. Canada Direct). It recommended that you not make calls abroad from hotels as these charge guests up to $4 US, even for collect and toll-free calls. Local calls from hotels can cost up to 3 pesos per call, while at phone booths they cost 50 centavos.

In addition, be wary of the service *Larga Distancia, To call the USA collect or with credit card Simply Dial 0* that is advertised throughout the bay area and at the airport. This business, which is also identified by a logo depicting a red maple leaf, sometimes confuses Canadian visitors who mistake it for Canada Direct. In reality it is a completely separate business, which charges exorbitant rates for every call. Calls to North America with this service cost no less than 23 pesos per minute and calls to Europe cost 27 pesos per minute, when the caller pays cash. Credit card payment is even more expensive.

Using a Foreign Operator

To call Canada:
Canada Direct: 95-800-010-1990 + area code + local number, or wait for an operator to help you.
AT&T: 95-800-010-1991 + area code + local number, or wait for an operator to help you.

To call the United States:
AT&T: 95-800-462-4240 + area code + local number, or wait for an operator to help you.
Sprint: 95-800-877-8000 + area code + local number, or wait for an operator to help you.
MCI: 95-800-674-7000 + area code + local number, or wait for an operator to help you.

To call Great Britain:
BT: 98-800-4400 (on dedicated phones)

Dialling Direct

To call North America, dial 00-1 + the area code + the local number.
For other international calls, dial 00 + country code + area code + local number.
For long-distance calls within Mexico, dial 0 + local number.

Country Codes

Australia	61
Belgium	32
Germany	49
Great Britain	44
Holland	31
Italy	39
New Zealand	64
Spain	34
Switzerland	41

Operator assistance

- for international calls, dial 09
- for calls within Mexico, dial 02
- for information, dial 04

 ACCOMMODATIONS

Except where otherwise indicated, it is unadvisable to drink tap water in hotels, as it is not purified. Unfortunately, most hotels do not provide purified water on the floors with guest rooms and take advantage of this inconvenience by selling bottled water in minibars. In Acapulco, so as not to bankrupt yourself on drinking water, you will have to replenish your water supply regularly at one of the stores along the bay. Also taking advantage of the water situation, some store-owners sell water at exorbitant prices, especially to tourists. The average price of a 1.5-litre bottle is 5.50 pesos. Be sure that the bottle is well sealed.

Rates

Large hotels, during the high season from December to May, often charge travellers without reservations rates that are completely exaggerated for the services rendered. As a general rule, in this period it is advisable to make reservations ahead of time through a travel agent. Travel agencies often organize airfare-hotel packages that prove far more economical than renting a room once arrived.

The prices indicated in the chart below are for the period from December to May **outside of the holidays** for a double-occupancy room, including 15% tax, **excluding** breakfast (except where otherwise indicated). From December 20th to January 10th, the prices below may be doubled or even tripled.

> $ = less than 200 pesos
> $$ = 200 to 400 pesos
> $$$ =400 to 800 pesos
> $$$$ = 800 to 1,500 pesos
> $$$$$ = more than 1,500 pesos

All-inclusive Packages in Acapulco

In recent years, a formula of all-inclusive holiday packages has become popular in Acapulco: for a fixed rate, for stays of one or two weeks, the hotel provides three meals per day and national drinks. This formula seems to be a good deal for the client, but it does have several disadvantages. Imagine having 21 meals in one week at the same restaurant. Usually the "all-inclusive" hotels offer two or three restaurants, but actually guests eat most meals in a cafeteria from a buffet table that does not vary much from day to day.

On the other hand, since restaurants are very inexpensive in Mexico, a budget for three meals per day outside the hotel, as well as for drinks, in American dollars would be as follows:

Breakfast $3 + Lunch $4 + Dinner $9 + Drinks $4 = $20

An all-inclusive package thus provides a savings of $140 US per week, hardly worth depriving oneself of the pleasure of the area's range of restaurants, of choosing where to eat every day according to your mood, and of the joy of discovery. Is the luxury of whimsy not one of the main reasons people travel? In fact, most guests at all-inclusive hotels go out at least a few times and spend part of their $140 savings anyway. It would be unthinkable not to visit a tropical nightclub like Tropicana (see p 101) at least once, or taste the Molcajete Acapulqueño at the traditional restaurant El Fogón (see p 93), without mentioning the very Mexican atmosphere that reigns on the Zócalo, where restaurants offer good cuisine at low prices (see p 94). Approximately 70 restaurants and over 20 night-clubs are described in this book and surely it is a delight to discover them.

For some, another major inconvenience of an all-inclusive package is that most guests tend to spend all day at the hotel, and staff organize activities for them that are often disruptive and noisy... while you are reading on your balcony, such as pool aerobics, volleyball tournaments, or dance competitions with blaring American music. Most of the time these activities have nothing at all to do with the Mexico travellers come to discover.

 RESTAURANTS

Prices described below refer to a meal for one person, including an appetizer, an entrée, and dessert. Tax is included in the prices, but service and drinks are not. The rule for tipping is to leave between 10% and 15%.

$ = less than 80 pesos
$$ = 80 to 120 pesos
$$$ = 120 to 200 pesos
$$$$ = 200 to 300 pesos
$$$$$ = over 300 pesos

Tipping

The term *propina incluida* signifies that the gratuity is included in the price. Usually, it is not included, and, depending on the quality of service, diners must budget for 10% to 15% of the total. Contrary to the practice in Europe, the tip is not included in the total, but rather must be calculated and remitted to the waiter by the diner. Service and tip are one and the same thing in North America.

MEXICAN CUISINE

Tortillas, tacos, empanadas, enchiladas, so many terms can be confusing to those encountering Mexican cuisine for the first time. Since prejudices die hard (dishes are too spicy, for example), too often visitors faced with new, unfamiliar flavours opt for international cuisine. Although some local dishes can prove particularly spicy, Mexican cuisine offers an infinite variety of dishes, from the mildest to the hottest. As a guide through the delicious meanderings of Mexican cuisine, we have assembled a gastronomic glossary below.

Ceviche	Raw shrimp, tuna or sea pike, "cooked" only in lime juice.
Chicharrón	Fried pork rind, usually served with the apéritif.
Chile	Fresh or dried peppers (there are more than 100 varieties) that are prepared in a thousand different ways: stuffed, or as stuffing, boiled, fried, etc.
Empanadas	Thin corn pancakes in the shape of turnovers, stuffed with meat, poultry or fish.
Enchiladas	Similar to rolled crepes made of corn flour, enchiladas are generally stuffed with chicken (less frequently with tuna), covered with a spicy sauce, sliced onions and cream, the whole sprinkled with cheese.

Guacamole   Salted and peppered purée of avocado mixed with diced tomatoes, onions, fresh peppers and a bit of lime juice. Even when this dish is not on the menu, do not hesitate to ask for *guacamole con totopos* (with corn chips), a very common dish that constitutes a refreshing appetizer or snack.

Mole   This term designates a category of creamy sauces composed of mixtures of spices, nuts, chocolate, tomatoes, *tortillas*, peppers, onions, and other foodstuffs varying by region. The most famous of these are Mole Poblano and Mole Negro Oaxaqueno, both based on chocolate and spices. These sauces accompany poultry and meat.

Peppers

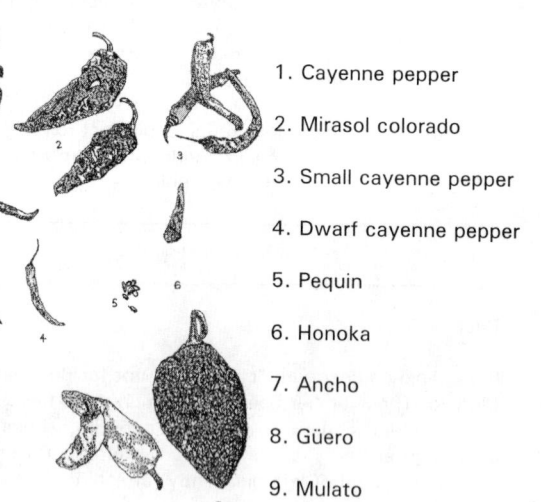

1. Cayenne pepper
2. Mirasol colorado
3. Small cayenne pepper
4. Dwarf cayenne pepper
5. Pequin
6. Honoka
7. Ancho
8. Güero
9. Mulato

Nopales	Cactus leaves (without the spines of course!) cooked in water or served in a soup or salad. The juice of these is also offered at breakfast.
Pozole	A corn and pork stew with radish, onion, coriander and lime juice. There are two varieties, red and green. The red is hotter.
Quesadillas	A sort of crepe stuffed with cheese and cream.
Tacos	A sort of rolled corn crepe often stuffed with chicken, but also frequently with other preparations.
Tamales	Corn husks stuffed with meat, poultry, or fish, mixed with bacon drippings and corn purée. Many vegetables and spices are also added to the stuffing, varying according to region.
Tortillas	As opposed to Spanish *tortillas* (made with eggs and potatoes), Mexican tortillas are flat pancakes with a corn-flour base, cooked on an unoiled griddle. Generally they accompany other dishes.
Totopos	These are a rough equivalent to North American potato chips. Made with corn here, they may be round or triangular.

Mexican Drinks

Beer

If you enjoy a beer with "character", opt for **Bohemia** or **Negro Modelo**. These amber beers have much more flavour than the pale ales and constitute excellent apéritifs. Those who only enjoy lighter beers will find the very famous **Corona** and the less known **Santa Clara** pleasantly refreshing.

Wine

In most cases, the least expensive wine served in restaurants is Mexican. Half-bottles are almost unheard-of on wine lists.

Budget for 75 pesos for a bottle of Mexican wine, 95 pesos to 110 pesos for a Chilean wine, and from 180 to 295 pesos for French wine. Given storage conditions and the climate here, it is recommended to drink local wine, which is also a nice way to taste the fruit of the local earth.

Agave

Apéritifs and *Digestifs*

The queen of the apéritifs, the **Margarita** makes people who drink immoderately lose their heads very quickly. It consists of a mixture of lime juice, Tequila, triple sec and sugar-cane syrup, all of it mixed with crushed ice, and poured into a glass with a salted rim. **Tequila**, produced in the lovely State of Jalisco, is squeezed from the bulbous base of the agave, a plant indigenous to Mexico. The juice collected is then slowly fermented producing a dry, white alcohol. Traditionally, tequila is drunk immediately after eating a pinch of salt. The **Piña Colada**, already world-famous, is a mixture of rum, coconut and pineapple juice.

 SHOPPING

In Mexico, shops are usually open from 9am to 8pm or 9pm, Monday to Saturday. However, in much-frequented towns like Acapulco and Taxco, some stores are open on Sunday and some are even open 24 hours a day (mainly larger stores). In general, prices are lower further from touristy areas. In Acapulco, stores in the entire neighbourhood near the Zócalo have much lower prices than those bordering the Costera.

Mexico has a reputation for its exceptionally colourful and rich variety of craft products. Acapulco and Taxco are no exceptions, and shoppers have little trouble finding whatever they seek here. We have listed interesting shopping ideas in the "Shopping"sections of each chapter.

Taxes

The local sales tax is called the "IVA" and is almost always included in prices.

 FESTIVALS AND HOLIDAYS

In Mexico, several Christian festivals are official holidays. In addition to these, there are a number of other celebrations that

are steeped in more local character. Some of the major festivities in Acapulco and Taxco are described below.

Acapulco

The Processions to Santa María de Guadalupe

From the 1st to the 11th of December in Acapulco, while townspeople are busy decorating the city, every day a procession files along the Costera to the Zócalo. Every athletic or cultural organization, every neighbourhood association, every business, and many other organizations makes its own procession, which, after reaching the Zócalo (also called "Plaza Alvarez"), enters Catedral Nuestra Señora de la Soledad to be blessed. Do not be surprised to see a float in honour of the Virgin draped with a large advertisement for Coca-Cola or a local nightclub! Lightheartedly following behind these floats, the employees of the represented firms sing the *Himno a Santa María de Guadalupe* while fireworks explode overhead in an unbelievable cacophony of crashes. These processions attain their height the night of December 11th. The first processions begin in the early evening and the last do not leave before 3am, followed by revellers emptying the nightclubs, and gay paraders, who are the last to be blessed by the priest (*Dios quiere a todo...*)! While these processions take place all over the country, here they don an especially entertaining character.

Finally, the 12th of December marks the most important holiday in Mexico (almost more important than the national holiday): the **Feast day of the Virgin of Guadalupe**. Pilgrims come by the tens of thousands to the basilica in Mexico City to see the famous wrap emblazoned with the image of the Virgin. According to popular belief, in 1531, this cloth was given by the Virgin herself to an Aztec peasant named Juan Diego, as proof to counter his lack of faith.

Taxco

The 1st of December is a special day in Taxco, the setting of an important fair: the *Feria de la Plata*. On this occasion, exhibitions are mounted all over the city presenting a unique

opportunity to view some of the most beautiful silversmith work in the world.

January 18th, parades are held to mark the feast day of Taxco's patron saint, Santa Prisca.

During Holy Week, many tourists come to Taxco to witness remarkable representations of the Passion.

MISCELLANEOUS

Electricity

Local electricity operates at 110 volts AC, as in North America. Plugs have two flat pins, so Europeans will need both a converter and a wall socket adapter.

Women Travellers

Women travelling alone in these cities should not have any problems. In general, locals are friendly and not too aggressive. Although men treat women with respect and harassment is relatively rare, Mexicans will undoubtedly flirt with female travellers—politely, though. Of course, a minimum amount of caution is required; for example, women should avoid walking alone through poorly lit areas at night. Furthermore, wearing clothes that are not too revealing will probably spare you some aggravation in this primarily Catholic country.

Time Zones

Puerto Vallarta is one hour behind Eastern Standard Time, six hours behind Greenwich Mean Time and seven hours behind continental Europe.

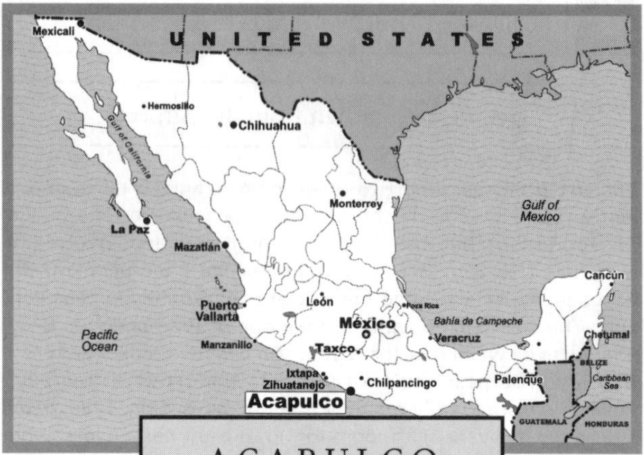

ACAPULCO

Imagine some 15 golden sandy beaches nestled in the curve of a bay surrounded by an imposing chain of mountains, the Sierra Madre del Sur. Now picture the same heavenly setting but with scores of luxurious hotels set right on the beach amidst luxurious vegetation. Throw in an infinite number of restaurants ready to delight even the most refined palate with flavours from all over the world, then top it all off with a vibrant nightlife that doesn't seem to wind down until the sun comes up. And there you have it: Acapulco! Although rivalled by the recently developed tourist areas on the coast of the Yucatán, Acapulco is still Mexico's most internationally renowned resort and attracts over a million tourists every year. And for a very good reason: as the local tourist brochures will tell you, the sun shines 360 days a year here. With its long bay, which stretches 16 kilometres, the "pearl of the Pacific" can satisfy visitors looking for action as well as those seeking a peaceful place to relax. As for those travellers with a yen for cultural activities, they can not only visit Acapulco's handful of museums and colonial vestiges, but also escape to the beautiful town of Taxco, a jewel of the colonial era, located less than three hours' drive away.

FINDING YOUR WAY AROUND

Getting Downtown from the Airport

The trip from the airport to downtown Acapulco takes about half an hour by car. Technically, it is possible to take public transportation, but the trip is a long one and involves a transfer. This option is not recommended for people with baggage, especially since the risk of being robbed is considerable. The best alternative is to take one of the numerous taxis or *colectivos* waiting at the exit of the airport. It costs between 150 and 185 pesos to take a taxi to the centre of the bay, while a *colectivo* only costs 38 pesos per person. *Colectivos* are simply minivans with room for up to eight passengers, who are dropped off right at their hotel. Although travelling by *colectivo* is cheap and relatively comfortable, some people might find it trying, particularly during the high season, when there is lots of pushing and shoving.

As the various means of transportation are strictly controlled at the airport, you have to pay at a stand near the exit. You'll be given a ticket, which you then give to the driver; no further payment is necessary, other than a small tip for handling your baggage. It should be noted that most air hotel packages include the transfer between the airport and the hotel.

From Downtown to the Airport

Getting back to the airport is an entirely different story, as the fare for a regular taxi is significantly lower, at around 70 pesos. It is therefore more economical to choose this option rather than take a *colectivo*, especially when there are more than two of you.

By Car

In the old centre, near the Zócalo, the roads are particularly congested, which can make driving here quite a challenge at times. Furthermore, the risk of having your car broken into is

considerable. For these reasons, and especially since the city's main attractions are all very close to each other and easily accessible on foot, by taxi or by bus, we do not recommend renting a car if you are planning on spending your entire trip in Acapulco.

If you do want to rent an automobile, however, take note that the speed limit is 50 kph, and that traffic circles are known as *glorietas* here. For those arriving from other parts of Mexico, the city of Acapulco is accessible from the 200, along the coast, and from the 95D (a toll road commonly known as the Autopista del Sol) from Mexico City (368 km) or other points north.

By Taxi

Roaming the streets 24 hours a day in a frenzied (we are not exaggerating!) search for tourists, taxis are legion in Acapulco. As soon as you walk out of your hotel, they'll go as far as trailing behind you, trying to offer you their services; what a nightmare! Their insistence makes walking seem like some sort of indecent act! It is true that competition is stiff in Acapulco, and that the tourist season is the only profitable time of the year for some drivers. While strolling around the bay, therefore, be prepared to hear this cheerful refrain: "*Taxi Amigo*"! Tiring as this might be the thousandth time, there's no denying that taxis are the most efficient means of getting around. There are no meters, so the drivers charge a fixed rate, which depends not only on your destination but also on where you are picked up. For example, a taxi taken straight from your hotel will cost more than one hailed along the Costera (also see p 38).

Sample fares:

From Playa Icacos to:

Puerto Marqués	30 pesos
Airport	60 pesos
Zócalo	20 pesos
Playa Condesa	12 pesos
Pie de la Cuesta	50 pesos
Estrella de Oro Terminal	20 pesos

By Bus

Acapulco's numerous public buses travel all around the bay. Though dilapidated and short on comfort, they are a typical and economical means of getting around. It costs only two pesos to go anywhere around the bay or to Pie de la Cuesta (four pesos for Bahía Marqués, since you have to transfer). There are public bus stops, marked by a blue sign and sometimes even a bus shelter, all along the Costera. For some obscure reason, some buses move quickly from one stop to the next, while others creep along almost at walking speed and stop anywhere they are asked to. Unfortunately, there is no real way to tell the difference between the two. If you are in a hurry, therefore, it is best to take a taxi. Finally, avoid taking buses when you are carrying baggage, as they are often packed, increasing your chances of getting robbed.

A few bus routes:

Base-Caleta: Along the Costera from the Icacos military base to Playa Caleta, by way of the Zócalo.

Base-Cine Río-Caleta: Same destination as the Base-Caleta bus, but via Avenida Cuauhtémoc and Wilfrido Massieu, passing the Estrella de Oro bus terminal along the way.

Although these destinations are marked on each vehicle, they are hand-written on the windshield in white letters and are therefore usually either illegible or visible only at the last moment.

By Scooter

Seldom used and unfortunately quite expensive here, scooters are one of the most pleasant means of getting around in the tropics. However, those riding them should be particularly cautious, as motorists here have little respect for either motorcyclists or pedestrians.

Rentals

Scooter rentals *(50 pesos/hour or 180 pesos/day)*

At the entrance of the Plaza Bahía shooping centre (next to the Acapulco Plaza hotel)
☎ 85-93-04

By Private Coach

Estrella de Oro is an extremely efficient company, and its buses are equipped with toilets. Some of the vehicles have televisions, and you might even find a free coffee dispenser on board. Possible destinations include Chilpancingo (the capital of the State of Guerrero), Taxco, Cuernavaca, Mexico City and Ixtapa-Zihuatanejo.

Unfortunately, for some unknown reason, the Estrella de Oro company doesn't sell return tickets, so each ticket must be purchased at the station from which you are leaving. As the seats are numbered, during the high season and on weekends it is best to reserve yours ahead of time, especially if you want a specific seat or wish to avoid jostling with the crowds. It is also wise to purchase your return ticket as soon as you arrive at your destination.

El Terminal Estrella de Oro
Av. Cuauhtémoc 158 *(at the corner of Wilfrido Massieu)*
Take any bus labelled "Base-Cine Río-Caleta"
☎ 85-87-05

 PRACTICAL INFORMATION

Tourist Information

Secretaría de Fomento Turístico del Estado de Guerrero
Information on the State of Guerrero and the city of Acapulco
La Costera 187 *(between the Zócalo and Parque Papagayo)*
☎ 86-91-67, 86-91-64 or 86-91-71 ext. 25
≠ 86-91-63

Asistencia Turística
Tourist assistance provided in various foreign languages.
☎ 84-45-83 or 84-44-16

Procuraduría del Turista
Problems or complaints
La Costera 4455 *(beside the Centro de Convenciones)*
☎ 84-44-16 or 84-45-83

Excursions

As you stroll along the bay, you'll see numerous little stalls, set up right on the sidewalk, offering all sorts of excursions and activities. These range from boat rides to tours of the islands. You can also purchase passes for discotheques or even buy a piece of property from these vendors! Bear in mind, however, that some of these outfits, especially those whose vendors approach you right on the street, are shady operations whose tickets aren't likely to be worth anything in exchange. To stay on the safe side, we strongly recommend dealing directly with one of the many agencies inside the local hotels. That way, if you are not satisfied with your purchase, you can always protest vigorously to the hotel or even file a complaint with the Procuraduría del Turista. Furthermore, as the hotels have lots of room to negotiate, their rates are no more expensive than those offered by external agencies. As far as the excursions themselves are concerned, most are cruises around the bay and organized tours in Taxco, Oaxaca and Mexico City.

The Bay of Acapulco and Area

Among the various excursions, you can take a moonlit boat ride *(about 300 pesos, buffet and drinks included)*, go to Isla Roqueta for a swim in the limpid waters of Playa Caleta *(15 pesos)*, explore the unspoiled beaches of Pie de la Cuesta and take a dip in the immense Laguna de Coyuca, located right nearby *(300 pesos including lunch with drinks)*, or simply take a tour of the city *(130 pesos)*. Bird-lovers might be interested in taking an ecological trip to the Laguna de Las Tres Palos, located right near the airport. Almost all the aforementioned outings are hosted by guides who speak both Spanish and English.

Elsewhere in the Country

Most tours starting in Acapulco are limited to three cities: Mexico City (the capital), Taxco (the silver city) and Oaxaca, home of the famous Monte Albán and Mitla sites. A few of these tours are briefly described below.

Taxco: This is the most popular tour destination and also the one closest to Acapulco. A marvellous colonial city nestled in the mountains (see p 119), Taxco is only three and a half hours' drive from Acapulco. In addition to admiring the local silver, you can visit one of the loveliest baroque churches in Mexico, Santa Prisca. Though this excursion need not take more than a day *(about 450 pesos for a guided tour)*, it is preferable to stay here at least one night to really soak up the local atmosphere *(about 1,500 pesos for a two-day excursion with meals and accommodations)*.

Oaxaca: The airline Aerocaribe (a subsidiary of Mexicana) has recently started organizing day trips to Oaxaca and the extraordinary Mitla and Monte Albán archaeological sites. There are departures from the Juan N. Alvarez international airport every day at 7am; the return flight leaves the same day at 10:50pm. Three different options are available: a tour of the colonial city of Oaxaca and the Monte Albán site, a tour of the Mitla and Monte Albán sites and a tour of Monte Albán only. All packages include round-trip air transportation, the services of a bilingual (English-Spanish) guide, one meal and admission to the various sites and museums *(between 1,265 and 1,365 pesos depending on the package)*.

Mail and Telegrams

Mexpost
La Costera 215 *(near Sanborn's and the old city)*
Mon to Fri 9am to 6pm, Sat 9am to 1pm

Useful Telephone Numbers

The area code for **Acapulco** is **74**.

Police: ☎ 85-06-50 or 85-08-62

In the event of an emergency (ambulance, fire department, police), dial **06**.

Airport: ☎ 66-94-29 *(every day 8am to 11pm; information on arrivals and departures).*

Hospitals

Hospital del Pacífico
Calle Fraile y Nao 4 (opposite the Iglesia Cristo Rey)
La Bocana
☎ 87-71-80

Hospital Privado Magallanes
Wilfrido Massieu 2
☎ 85-65-44, 85-67-06 or 85-65-97

Pharmacies

Farmacia America
Calle Horacio Nelson 40 *(near the Baby'O discotheque)*
☎ 84-52-32

Farmacias EMY
La Costera *(opposite the Paraiso Acapulco hotel, near Parque Papagayo)*
24 hours a day
☎ 85-98-86 and 86-17-55

Newspapers and Television

American tourists won't have any trouble finding newspapers from home and can even see the latest American news broadcasts (especially in big hotels). Visitors who understand Spanish can keep up with international current events on the Spanish channel, 38, every day at 7pm. This news program is broadcasted especially for Latin America.

Banks

There are banks all along the Costera, and you'll have no trouble making withdrawals or exchanging currency. Among the larger banks, Banamex and Bancomer both have automated tellers where you can make cash withdrawals with your credit card or bank card (Cirrus or Plus).

Airlines

Continental Airlines
At the airport only
9am to 5pm
☎ 66-90-63 or 66-90-46, toll-free within Mexico
☎ 91-800-900-50

Delta
At the airport only
☎ 66-94-81 or 66-94-05, toll-free within Mexico
☎ 91-800-901-22

American Airlines
At the airport only
☎ toll-free within Mexico 91-800-904-60

Taesa
La Costera 512-2
☎ 86-56-00 or at the airport 66-90-67, toll-free within Mexico
☎ 91-800-904-63

Mexicana
La Costera 1252
☎ 84-16-79 or at the airport 66-91-21, toll-free within Mexico
☎ 91-800-502-20

Aeromexico
La Costera 286
☎ 85-16-00 or at the airport 66-91-09, toll-free within Mexico
☎ 91-800-909-99

Sample air fares from Acapulco (as of December 1996, one-way):

Mexico City	423 pesos
Oaxaca	402 pesos
Guadalajara	759 pesos
Cuernavaca	150 pesos
Puerto Vallarta	659 pesos
Mérida	774 pesos
Cancún	1,307 pesos

 EXPLORING

Commonly known as the (La) Costera, broad **Avenida Costera Miguel Alemán (1)** runs all the way around the Bay of Acapulco. It is lined with highrise hotels whose rooms offer magnificent views of the bay, and by an impressive string of powdery beaches that are the delight of swimmers. Among the best-known, from east to west, are **Playa Icacos**, **Playa Condesa**, **Hornitos** and **Hornos**, and **Playas Tamarindo** and **Dominguillo**. **Playas Manzanillo**, **Honda** and **Larga**, for their part, mark the base of the Las Playas peninsula, at the west tip of the bay. Next, on the peninsula itself, come **Playas Caleta** and **Caletilla**. Finally, on the island of the same name, **Playa Roqueta** tops off this long list, which is still far from exhaustive.

The Costera itself is a bustling artery swarming with taxis and noisy old buses at all hours. Be particularly careful when crossing this street, as there are few traffic lights on it and the cars move along at a good clip. Despite the pollution created by this endless stream of automobiles, visitors who like lots of action will be delighted by the many stores, restaurants, bars, hotels, discotheques and all sorts of other establishments here. Though you will be relentlessly pursued by taxis, go ahead and walk up and down this long avenue; doing so is one of the best ways to explore Acapulco. Watch out for the holes and various obstacles littering the sidewalks, though.

CICI (Centro Internacional de Convivencia Infantil) (2) *(admission fee; every day 10am to 6pm; La Costera, near Calle Cristóbal Colón and the Hard Rock Café)* The various swimming pools (including a wave pool), water slides, restaurants,

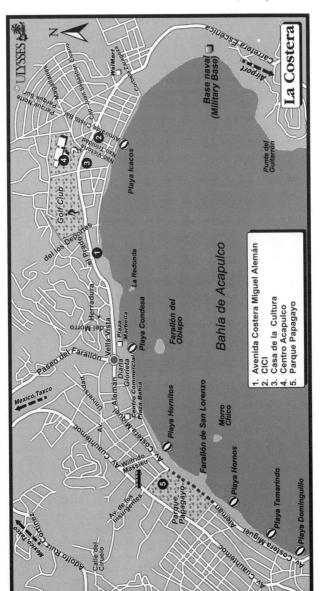

La Costera

1. Avenida Costera Miguel Alemán
2. CICI
3. Casa de la Cultura
4. Centro Acapulco
5. Parque Papagayo

Bahía de Acapulco

Base naval (Military Base)

Airport

Carretera Escénica

Punta del Guitarrón

Playa Icacos

Golf Club

del los Deportes

Av. Prados

La Redonda

Farallón del Obispo

Playa Condesa

Plaza Marbella

del Morro

Herradura

Vella Vista

Paseo del Farallón

Diana Glorieta

Centro Commercial

Plaza Bahía

Mexico, Taxco

Av. Wilfrido Massieu

Farallón de San Lorenzo

Morro Chico

Playa Hornitos

Playa Hornos

Parque Papagayo

Av. Cuauhtémoc

Av. Costera Miguel Alemán

Playa Tamarindo

Playa Dominguillo

Av. de los Insurgentes

Calle del Ciruelo

Mexico, Taxco

Adolfo Ruiz Cortines

Universidad

Wal-Mart

Parque Norte

Parque Sur

cafeterias and seal and dolphin show here are sure to be a hit with children. The kids can entertain themselves safely while their parents enjoy the pleasant surroundings in the shade of the palm trees.

Located near the Centro de Convenciones, or Centro Acapulco, the **Casa de la Cultura (3)** *(La Costera, near the CICI)* is simply a series of small modern buildings containing various galleries where works by local artists are exhibited and sold. These are surrounded by a pretty garden with a library and an outdoor theatre in the middle.

The imposing **Centro Acapulco (4)**, also known as the **Centro de Convenciones** *(La Costera, northwest of the CICI complex)*, designed for conventions and cultural events (see "Entertainment", p 99) will be of interest mainly to fans of modern architecture. Surrounded by fountains and gardens, it also contains shops, restaurants, movie theatres, a crafts centre and a theatre where folk shows are presented.

If you'd like to cool down in the shade of some lovely trees, head to **Parque Papagayo ★ (5)** *(every day 10am to 6pm; La Costera, near Playa Hornitos)*, where you can admire exotic birds, big turtles and miniature replicas of *Naos de China*, the famous Spanish galleons once built in the bay (not open to the public). Unfortunately, the park is not in the best shape and could use a good cleaning. The presence of an old cablecar and a chairlift, both of which have fallen out of use, further accentuates the park's state of neglect. Possible activities include renting a pedalboat or going to the amusement park *(Mon to Fri 3:30pm to 10:30pm, Sat and Sun 3pm to 11pm)*.

Located right next to the old city, the **Fuerte San Diego ★★★ (6)** is the city's most impressive colonial vestige, and as such merits a visit. Erected in the early 17th century, it was completely destroyed by a violent earthquake in 1776. Reconstructed in 1778, it enabled the Spanish to protect their precious cargoes of Asian (mainly Filipino) goods against repeated attacks by English and Dutch pirates. A century later, the fort was used by Republican troops fighting for independence. Its Vauban-style double wall has been beautifully restored and is in perfect condition. Unfortunately, there is not a single picnic table to be found here. Before entering the heart of the fortress, it is pleasant to stroll around the rampart walk and

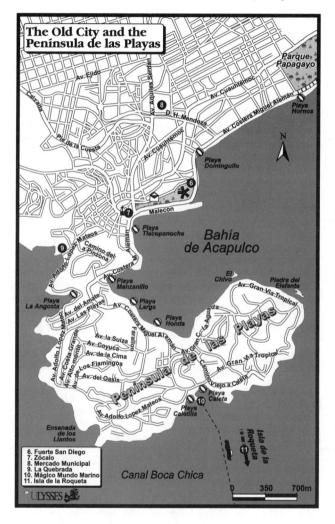

The Old City and the Península de las Playas

Parque Papagayo

Av. Ejido

Calzada

Av. Aquiles Serdán

Av. Cuauhtémoc

D. H. Mendoza

Pie de la Cuesta

Av. Cuauhtémoc

Av. Costera Miguel Alemán

Playa Hornos

N

Playa Domingullo

Malecón

Playa Tlacopanoche

Bahía de Acapulco

Av. Adolfo López Mateos

Camino de la Pinzona

Av. Costera

Playa Manzanillo

Playa Larga

Playa Honda

El Chivo

Av. Gran Vía Tropical

Piedra del Elefante

Playa La Angosta

Av. del Amate

Av. las Playas

Av. Costera Miguel Alemán

Av. Costera Farallón

Av. la Suiza

Av. Goyuca

Av. de la Cima

Av. de los Flamingos

Av. del Oasis

Av. Costa Grande

Av. Alta-monte

Península de las Playas

Av. Gran C. La Agua...

Camino Viejo a Caleta

Av. Gran Vía Tropical

Playa Caleta

Av. Adolfo López Mateos

Playa Caletilla

Ensenada de los Llantos

6. Fuerte San Diego
7. Zócalo
8. Mercado Municipal
9. La Quebrada
10. Mágico Mundo Marino
11. Isla de la Roqueta

Canal Boca Chica

Isla de la Roqueta

0   350   700m

© ULYSSES

take in a general view of the structure. Be careful, though: in certain places, the passage is narrow. After making a full circle, you'll arrive opposite the footbridge leading into the fort, which now houses the remarkable **Museo Histórico de Acapulco ★★★** *(14 pesos, free admission Sun; Tue to Sun 10:30 to 5pm, no one admitted after 4:40pm; entrance on the Costera, opposite the old docks, just past the Las Parrillas restaurant)*, an absolute must. Set aside an afternoon to visit this museum, which offers a wealth of information on the city's history and its trade relations with Asia. In some rooms, the commentary is written in both English and Spanish, in others only in Spanish.

Among the many objects on display are some magnificent pieces of Chinese porcelain and an interesting model of the famous *Nao de China* ships. Built in Acapulco, these ships should have been called *Galeons de Filipinas*, as the first place they docked was the Philippines. Furthermore, it was with that country that the great commercial romance between Asia and Spain began, silk being the most sought-after merchandise in Europe at the time.

After touring the museum, make sure to go up to the roof of the fort, where you can take in a splendid view of the bay and the Las Playas peninsula.

Even if you're pressed for time, don't forget to visit the **Zócalo ★ (7)**, the old city's central square, also known as Plaza Juan Alvarez. This pleasant square, of little architectural interest, except perhaps for the **Nuestro Señora de la Soledad** cathedral (it would be hard to define the style of its strange-looking dome), is worth visiting mainly for its convivial atmosphere. Take the time to sip a cup of coffee in the shade of the numerous trees around the square so that you can observe all the activity taking place here. The Zócalo is a popular meeting place for Mexicans, and shoe-shiners can be seen at work here and there, chatting away with their customers. It is well worth taking the time to stroll through the maze of little streets around the square. You'll find yourself surrounded by some pretty chaotic architecture, but if it's authenticity you're looking for, this working-class Mexican neighbourhood is fascinating. In addition to scores of little shops, restaurants and bistros, some more tasteful than others, but all full of local colour, you can explore the famous **Mercado Municipal ★ (8)**

(right next to Avenida Diego Hurtado Mendoza, between Avenida Cuauhtémoc and Avenida Aquiles Serdán). This is one of the most entertaining attractions in town and a must-see for those who enjoy mingling with the crowd (see also "Shopping", p 105).

You can't leave magical Acapulco without having seen the famous *clavadistas* in action at least once. The road known as **La Quebrada ★★ (9)** *(Plaza Las Glorias, west of the Zócalo, opposite the Las Glorias hotel)* leads to the top of the cliffs where you can watch athletic Mexicans diving into the Pacific from heights of 25 to 35 metres. These feats are not performed, however, without a divine blessing, and the divers take the plunge only after paying a short visit to the Virgen de Guadalupe to ask for her protection. Though the swimmers seem to be taking these dangerous leaps for the sheer pleasure of doing so, the activity has long since become purely commercial. The Las Glorias hotel is among the most sought-after places from which to watch the divers, but you'll have to pay 61 pesos (which includes two domestic drinks) to ensconce yourself on the panoramic terrace and take in the spine-tingling spectacle. For a better view, go to the **Las Clavadistas** terrace *(10 pesos; diving schedule: 12:45pm, 7:30pm, 8:30pm, 9:30pm, 10:30pm)*, located below, right across from where the divers plunge into the sea. The terrace was laid out by the *clavadistas* union, and the profits go to a pension fund for the divers. The admission fee does not include any drinks, but you can easily buy one from one of the many vendors that frequent the spot. If you go to the 12:45 session, make sure to protect yourself from the sun, as there is no shade here.

The Zócalo also offers access to the pleasant Gran Vía Tropical scenic highway, which runs around part of the Las Playas peninsula. In addition to affording some magnificent views, the road will take you to the **Mágico Mundo Marino (10)** *(20 pesos, children 3 to 12 15 pesos; every day 9am to 7pm; between Playas Caleta and Caletilla)*, whose unsightly architecture and colours unfortunately detract somewhat from the setting. This water park is sure to be a hit with children and adults alike. In addition to seeing various dolphin and seal shows, you can take a close look at some sharks and pirahnas. You'll also find water slides and swimming pools (no predators here!), as well as a restaurant with outdoor seating.

There are a number of excursions from La Caleta and La Caletilla beaches to **Isla de la Roqueta (11)**. Many local agencies offer crossings aboard glass-bottomed boats, so that you can admire (or so they claim) the magnificent sea bed and the amazing **Capilla Submarina**. This curious chapel, over seven metres underwater, houses **La Virgen de Guadelupe**, a statue of the Virgin Mary, which seems to be languishing there, waiting to be pulled up for her annual cleaning. Unfortunately, more often than not, the magnificent sea bed that you've heard so much about is barely visible. A return trip to the island aboard a glass-bottomed boat costs 25 pesos; aboard a standard boat, 15. Visitors are let off on the island and can stroll about or take a swim before getting back on the boat. The last trip back is at 5pm.

BEACHES

This section contains a brief description of all the major beaches in the Bay of Acapulco. As each has a character of its own, travellers will have no trouble finding one that suits them. However, every enjoyable activity has a down side: wherever you decide to daydream, always bear in mind that the sea can be treacherous. The greatest caution should be exercised in the water, and unseasoned swimmers should avoid venturing out too far. Another hazard to take into consideration is the harmful effect that the sun can have on skin. For a nice, painless tan, don't forget to protect yourself regularly with a sunscreen suited to your needs. Sunglasses and a hat will also come in handy.

The beaches described below are listed from east to west:

Playa Icacos ★★★ The "sister beach" of the famous Playa La Condesa, Playa Icacos fronts more affluent areas than its neighbours to the west. The hotels here are also decidedly more modern, albeit not always in the best of taste. The wide, well-maintained beach is frequented by a select crowd of magazine models, well-bred exhibitionists and wealthy folk. All sorts of water sports can be enjoyed here, and you'll have no trouble emptying your wallet. This beach will appeal particularly to novice swimmers, as the surf is not as heavy here, and even gets relatively calm farther east, toward Punta Guitarrón. If you get up early in the morning, near the Copacabana hotel you can

watch the fishermen bringing in their nets full of fish, which are sold right on the beach.

Playa Condesa ★★: Numerous highrise hotels, scores of restaurants with outdoor seating and an impressive number of trendy bars await you at Playa La Condesa. If you like nonstop action, this place should be right up your alley. In the afternoon, the beach is quickly overrun by fun-loving sun-worshippers, while the cheerful cries of swimmers form a background noise that blends with the crashing of the waves. The two little islets opposite the beach seem to have been set there by Mother Nature as a treat for the eyes. Finally, as if to complete this picture-postcard setting, a host of boats ranging from the most modest of vessels to luxurious yachts parade by in the distance, with an azure sky strewn with colourful parachutes as a backdrop. Parasailing, scuba diving, waterskiing, windsurfing... anything is possible here. Come night-fall, the discotheques and hip nightclubs take over until the wee hours, and the rules of conduct can be summed up in two words: pleasure and relaxation.

Playas Hornos and **Hornitos:** These two beaches, located side by side, are a more modest version of the highly popular Playa Condesa. Thronged in the afternoon, these beaches welcome a less affluent crowd of Mexicans and travellers on a limited budget. Beach-goers can enjoy numerous restaurants and water sports here at reasonable prices. The part of the beach in front of Parque Papagayo, frequented mainly by Mexican families, is very pleasant, as there are no big buildings along it and it is far from the noisy Costera.

Playa Honda and **Playa Larga:** Stretching from the old city to the base of the Las Playas peninsula, these two beaches serve mainly as the starting point for various excursions, including deep-sea fishing trips. It is pleasant to stroll along them, watching the boats coming and going and admiring all the luxurious yachts.

Playa Caleta and **Playa Caletilla:** Located on the Las Playas peninsula, these two little beaches are slightly removed from the urban centre. The sand is fine and the water as calm and limpid as can be. A number of excursions to Isla Roqueta are offered here, and the place is perfect for scuba diving and other related sports. The Magíco Mundo water park (see Exploring,

p 67) is located between the two beaches, making the area very popular with Mexican families, especially on weekends and during school holidays. If you're looking for peace and quiet, avoid this spot during those periods.

Playa Roqueta: Located on the island of the same name, this beach will appeal mainly to those looking for a relatively peaceful spot, except on weekends and during school holidays, when it is literally overrun with Mexican families. Limpid water and fine sand scattered with a few boulders await you here.

 OUTDOOR ACTIVITIES

The most important seaside resort in Mexico must, of course, offer visitors a whole panoply of outdoor activities, but Acapulco has never turned toward the surrounding forests and mountains, and the absence of mountain hiking and horseback-riding trails in the forest is lamentable. Outdoor activities in Acapulco are directed exclusively toward the sea.

To get closer to nature, travellers go to Pie de la Cuesta, where hotel development is much more modest. For luxury sports, they opt for the golf courses and tennis courts of Bahía Marqués.

Those who enjoy the social aspect of sport congregate at Acapulco Bay, where they may take part in favourite activities in a generally cheerful and animated atmosphere. A multitude of agencies, the majority of which are located in the large hotels along the bay, propose various outdoor activities.

 Water-skiing

As at any self-respecting seaside resort, water-skiing is a major activity here. Although it is possible to go water-skiing in the bay, the best place to enjoy the sport is Laguna Coyuca (see p 111), as the large numbers of people swimming in the Bay of Acapulco make this activity dangerous.

Jet-skiing

Most of the agencies and hotels that rent out these contraptions are located along Playas Icacos, Condesa and Hornitos. To rent one, take a stroll on these beaches and shop around, just as you would for anything else. The prices vary considerably from one place to the next, so don't hesitate to bargain. Be prepared to pay between 160 and 180 pesos per half-hour or 320 pesos per hour. The rental fee is per jet-ski, not per person, so two can ride for the price of one, a more economical option that is just as much fun. Before speeding off, look around carefully for swimmers, as there are a lot of them here during the high season.

  Scuba Diving and Snorkelling

No need to be a scuba pro to go diving with **Acapulco Divers** *(9:30am, 11:30am and 2:30pm departures from Playa Icacos, in front of the La Palapa hotel)*. This diving school will provide you with all the necessary gear, as well as transportation and the services of a guide. The expeditions last two and a half hours, and the sites vary depending on how experienced the participants are. Those diving for the first time are taken near peaceful Isla Roqueta; experts out into the bay. Snorkelling equipment is available for the less adventurous. It costs about 235 pesos to go scuba diving and 117 pesos to go snorkelling.

 Parasailing

Many agencies and hotels along Playas Icacos and Condesa offer this type of activity. Parasailing is not risk-free however, and is not suitable for people with no head for heights, nor for those who have health problems and are on medication. Also, don't forget that drinking alcohol before going parasailing (or taking part in any other activity!) is highly inadvisable. If you heed these few rules, you'll have a lovely time floating over the bay for the sum of 100 pesos per 15 minutes.

Golf

In addition to being centrally located, the **Club de Golf Acapulco** *(La Costera, next to the Centro de Convenciones, ☎ 84-07-81)* is remarkably inexpensive. Greens fees run from 40 to 50 pesos for its nine- and 18-hole courses.

 Speedboating

Shotover Jet *(La Costera, Centro Comercial Marbella, local 4, CP 39690, ☎ 84-11-54, ⚎ 84-26-48)* takes thrill-seekers on tumultuous rides on the Río Papagayo, north of Acapulco; you have to take a bus ride of a little over an hour to get there. The owners promise you a rush of adrenalin aboard a boat that performs various stunts. After experiencing these New Zealand-style sensations (the company is based down under), you can catch your breath and return to the peaceful reality of the beaches in the bay. About 275 pesos per person (children 117 pesos), including round-trip transportation from the Costera.

 ACCOMMODATIONS

In order to make this chapter easier to read, we have used the short form "La Costera", often used by Acapulco residents, to refer to Avenida Miguel Alemán. Also, because the Bay of Acapulco is so long (16 km), we have divided it into five areas (see inside front cover), thus facilitating the task of locating the various establishments. From east to west, these five areas are **Playa Icacos, Playa Condesa, Playa Condesa to Playa Hornitos, Playa Hornos to the Zócalo** and the **Península de las Playas**.

Playa Icacos

El Tropicano (16) *($; ps, ≡, tv, ≈, ℜ; La Costera 510, near the Wal-Mart, ☎ 84-11-01, 84-11-00 or 84-13-32, ⚎ 84-13-08)*, located five minutes' walk from Playa Icacos, is a modest hotel whose charm lies in its lush garden filled with flowers and trees. All the rooms adjoin a small terrace that offers a view but little privacy (avoid those near the swimming pools). The

decor, for its part, could use some freshening up. Also, with 137 rooms in a relatively small space, this place is not the quietest, and is thus best suited to visitors who enjoy a lively atmosphere. Amenities include two small pools, a piano bar and a restaurant.

The **Hotel Marbella (27)** *($$; ps, ≡, tv, ≈, ℜ; Calle Horacio Nelson 2, behind the Baby-O discotheque, near the Wal-Mart, C.P. 39850, ☎ 84-29-43 or 84-28-90, ≈ 84-21-57, toll-free within Mexico ☎ 91-800-84-01-24)*, a modest little establishment with 44 rooms, deserves a special mention for its pleasant setting. Though the rooms don't offer a view of the bay, they face onto an attractive courtyard, which is shaded by trees, has a pool, and is secluded from the noise of the nearby Costera. The rooms are flooded with light and decorated in a modest but tasteful fashion. Though the common areas of many hotels are poorly kept, here they are prettily decorated with original paintings and earthenware jars set here and there. Excellent value.

The **Acasol (4)** *($$; ps, ≡, ≈; La Costera 53, near the Copacabana, ☎ 84-27-00, 84-02-55 or 84-68-67, ≈ 84-09-77)* is a modest little hotel with a small pool in the middle. The rooms are simple and clean, with a nondescript decor and neon lighting. Only a few have a balcony. The beach is just 150 metres away, and there is a shopping centre near by.

With its big, glassed-in entryway, the **Days Inn Acapulco (12)** *($$$; pb, ≡, K, ≈, tv, ℜ; La Costera 2310, opposite the Wal-Mart, C.P. 39840, ☎ 84-53-32 or 84-53-65, ≈ 84-58-22)* is quite impressive. When we were there, the building was undergoing a major overhaul and the rooms were being renovated. Part of the project was to equip each room with a kitchenette. Despite this freshening-up, the rooms still look somewhat outmoded, and the carpets and doors seem to have been fixed up a little too quickly! This hotel, too, is located perpendicular to the coast, 200 metres from the beach, so none of the rooms offer a full view of the sea. All rooms have a balcony, but with no furniture and no privacy. Ask for one on the left side of the building, with a view of the military base and Punte Diamante. Although a building that looks as if it will obstruct the view a little is presently under construction, the area on this side of the building is still fairly clear. The other side gives onto a group of buildings (including the new

Oceanico 2000 complex) stretching off into the distance, as well as a brand new discotheque with a tower designed to look like a keep. In addition to this striking feature, the discotheque has a revolving lighthouse that projects its beams right onto the neighbourhing buildings, proving that money and good taste don't always go together. Despite these drawbacks, the Days Inn offers good value near the beach, numerous services and nightspots. On the ground floor, guests have access to a cafeteria, a bar, a beauty salon, safes and shops.

Breaking the monotony of the big highrises in this area, the **Malibu (26)** *($$$; pb, ≡, tv, ≈; La Costera 20, C.P. 39690, opposite the golf club, ☎ 84-10-70, ⬄ 84-09-94, toll-free in the U.S. and Canada ☎ 1-800-446-2747)* is a modest-sized hotel with unusual architecture. Its originality lies in the design of its common areas, which are perfectly round and decorated with lots of trailing plants. These are surrounded by 80 suites in two buildings. All the rooms have a balcony, but only a few of those in Torre B offer a direct view of the sea. The modern decor of the rooms is lacking in warmth and is starting to show its age a bit. An attractive octagonal swimming pool, surrounded by palm trees, faces onto the beach. The relatively limited number of rooms makes this a good place for visitors looking for a more convivial atmosphere.

Visitors will have no trouble spotting the **Calinda Beach (16)** *($$$; pb, ≡, tv, ≈, ℜ; La Costera 1260, opposite the gold club, C.P. 39690, ⬄ 84-04-10, toll-free in the U.S. and Canada ☎ 1-800-221-2222, toll-free within Mexico ☎ 91-800-90-00, www.hotelchoice.com)*, the only perfectly round hotel in the bay. Its 350 rooms will be appreciated by those with a penchant for panoramic views; with a little luck, you'll get to enjoy a full view of the bay right from your balcony. Despite its amusing architecture and lovely view, the Calinda Beach is strangely devoid of charm. The rooms and common areas are not very tastefully decorated, and the furniture is strictly utilitarian, even depressing. Furthermore, the balconies are so close together that it is literally impossible to enjoy the use of your own with any real privacy. The tiny swimming pool is another drawback. Despite its flaws, however, this hotel can still claim the advantage of being located right on the beach and offering an unimpeded view. When this guide went to press, no buildings had yet spoiled its immediate surroundings.

Located on a hillside, the **Club Bananas Tropical (8)** *($$$; ps, ≡, ≈; Av. Monterrey 195, behind the golf club, C.P. 39690, ☎ 84-84-21, ≈ 84-73-44, toll-free within Mexico ☎ 91-800-09-410)* offers guests two choices: simple rooms with a small balcony (most with no privacy) or *casitas*, small apartment-style units with a large bathroom and two rooms able to accommodate up to four adults. The latter have a large private balcony and are located side by side in a series of two-story buildings. Whichever option you choose, the rates are all-inclusive, which has certain disadvantages (see p 44). The decor is attractive enough, but the individual air-conditioning units are a source of constant noise. None of the units offer a direct view of the sea or the bay. Two restaurants, one Italian (reservations required) and one buffet-style (very limited selection), and a bar can be found on the premises. With the bar alongside the pool and the discotheque, all right near the rooms, this place is not exactly a haven of peace and is thus best suited to those who like to party night and day. The hotel provides free shuttle service to Playa Francia *(every day 10am to 5pm)* and the Costera *(every day 9pm to 11pm)* every half-hour.

The **Copacabana (11)** *($$$; ps, ≡, ≈, tv, ℜ; Tabachines 2, near the Elcano hotel, C.P. 39360, ☎ 84-32-60 or 84-31-55, ≈ 84-62-68, toll-free in the U.S. and Canada ☎ 1-800-562-0197, toll-free within Mexico ☎ 91-800-09-888)*, set right on Playa Icacos, is an 18-story tower containing 422 large rooms, each with a minibar and a small balcony with a view of the sea and part of the bay. The decor of the rooms is inviting, if a bit outmoded. In addition to a swimming pool and a whirlpool, guests will find several shops, a bar and a fast-food service on the premises. Safes are also available at the front desk. Among the undeniable advantages of this place, its location, removed from the noisy Costera yet not too far from numerous restaurants, discotheques and shops, is worth taking into consideration.

The huge, 27-story **Hotel La Palapa (22)** *($$$; ps, ≡, ≈, tv, ℜ; La Costera 210, just east of the Days Inn, ☎ 84-55-18 or 84-53-63, ≈ 84-83-99)*, built right on Playa Icacos, is one of the local giants. Its imposing lobby boasts lovely Art Nouveau-style stained-glass windows, whose effect, unfortunately, is marred by the rest of the decor, which is rather chaotic and devoid of style. Like that of the common areas, the decor of

the 250 large suites appears to have seen better days. Orange and brown are the dominant colours. Each suite is equipped with a kitchenette and a refrigerator, but you have to pay extra to use them. A limited number of the suites offer a full view of the bay, and most of the private terraces are on either side of the central wing. For a relatively clear view, ask for a suite in the east wing, on the same side as the naval base. On the ground floor, guests have access to a bar, two restaurants and a swimming pool.

Though the lobby of the **Hyatt Regency (21)** *($$$$$; pb, ≡, ≈, tv, ℜ; La Costera 1, C.P. 39869, near the base, ☎ 869-1234, ≈ 843-087, toll-free in the U.S. and Canada ☎ 1-800-233-1234, toll-free within Mexico ☎ 91-800-00-500)* is uninviting, sombre and adorned with artificial palm trees (!), the rooms are tastefully decorated. The warm, cheerful colours of the fabrics and various handcrafted touches offer an elegant antidote to the coldness of the modern furnishings. The deluxe rooms, for their part, are noteworthy for their beautiful travertine bathrooms. Each room has a safe, and the hotel has its own water purification system. Here, too, only the suites offer a full view of the bay, and most of the other rooms are located at the building's extremities, thus offering a partial view of the bay or the mountain. A highrise is going up nearby, so make sure to ask for a room on the same side as the naval base. As far as the hotel's overall appearance is concerned, everything is well-ordered and sparkling clean, even sterile (there is not a single plant to be found in the long hallways). Two pools, three restaurants, three bars and a shopping arcade further enhance the Hyatt's already solid reputation. For a surcharge, guests can also enjoy the use of five tennis courts and a gym, all right near by.

Of the scores of hotels lining the Bay of Acapulco, the **Elcano (17)** *($$$$$; pb, tv, ≡, ⊗, ≈, ℜ, ☺; La Costera 75, C.P. 39840, opposite the golf club, ☎ 84-19-50, ≈ 84-22-30, toll-free in the U.S. and Canada ☎ 1-800-972-2162, toll-free within Mexico ☎ 91-800-09-075)* offers probably the best deal in its category. Named after sailor Sebastián Elcano (the first to circumnavigate the globe, thus completing a voyage begun with Magellan, who had died in the Philippines), the Elcano can pride itself on being one of the oldest hotels in the bay. As such, it boasts an outstanding site, facing directly onto the water at the mouth of the bay. Each room enjoys a lovely view

of the beach, the bay and the horizon over the Pacific. The building was elegantly renovated in 1991, but certain original elements, such as the monumental stairway leading to the pool, were preserved. The systematic use of blue and white throughout the hotel, in the common areas and guest rooms alike, is a reminder of how ubiquitous the sea is here. The rooms are decorated with paintings and lithographs by artist Cristina Rubalcava (see inset p 21), another indication of this establishment's level of sophistication. The tasteful furniture, with its simple lines, serves to heighten the airy feel of these rooms opening onto the sea. The bathrooms, for the most part, are equipped with a pretty, old-fashioned marble-topped wooden washstand. Each room also contains a safe. Most rooms have a private balcony with a direct view of the bay and elegant wooden furniture. The hallways facing onto the Costera are literally flooded with plants in order to camouflage the uninspiring view of this urban highway and also to stifle the noise coming from it. A small exercise room *(Mon to Fri 8am to 4pm, Sat until 7pm, Sun 2pm)*, a large, shallow pool *(every day 9am to 9pm)*, a bar and a pleasant restaurant (see p 89) round off the facilities at this extremely appealing place. Finally, visitors looking for the height of elegance will be interested to learn that the 20 penthouses and the honeymoon suite offer a view of both the sea and the mountains and have whirlpool baths on their balconies. Hot tub-lovers take note!

Playa Condesa

The **Panoramic (30)** *($$-$$$; ps, ≡, ≈, tv, ℜ; Av. Condesa 1; from the Costera, take Calle del Morro then the first right and follow the signs for the restaurant El Campanario, ☎ 84-07-24, 84-07-09 or 84-07-61, ≈ 84-86-39)* has 200 rooms in two terraced buildings set on a hillside, slightly removed from all the hustle and bustle. The rooms offer a panoramic view of the bay; those with the best vantage point are in the main buildings, where the reception desk is located. The rooms are attractively decorated and equipped with a safe. Each room has a balcony, but none of these are very private, as they give onto the terrace and swimming pool below. There are also two tennis courts and a small soccer field for sports buffs. The hotel is 500 metres from the beach. Attractive rates.

Picture two 30-story concrete towers rising up side by side into the sky. The **Torres Gemelas (38)** *($$$; ps, ≡, tv, K, ≈, ℜ; La Costera 1230, between Glorieta Diana and the golf club, ☎ 84-70-10, 84-46-45, 84-48-27 or 81-26-62, ⇥ 84-47-27)* contain 613 studios decorated in a nondescript fashion but equipped with all the necessities. Kitchenettes, direct access to the beach and a huge pool are among the pluses offered here. The place could use a fresh coat of paint, however. If you'd like a relatively unimpeded view, you should obviously steer clear of the studios facing the other tower.

If we were to choose one word to describe the decor of the **Romano Palace (37)** *($$$; ps, ≡, ≈, ℜ; La Costera 130, between the Glorieta Diana and the golf club, ☎ 84-77-30, ⇥ 84-13-50 and 84-79-95 toll-free within Mexico ☎ 91-800-09-800)*, it would have to be "kitschy" (its neighbour, the Tortuga, brightly coloured orange and blue, wins the prize, though!). After seeing the Roman mosaics in the fountain at the entrance and the frescoes of Roman chariots in the common areas, visitors will hardly be surprised to find a swimming pool surrounded by Greek columns and adorned here and there with effigies of David and the Venus de Milo! The building itself is purely 20th-century in style—a big tower containing 279 rooms, each with a balcony. Their decor, recently freshened up, follows the original style of the common areas, this time with an Oriental accent. The rooms face onto the noisy Costera and Playa Condesa, nicknamed Disco Beach—and with good reason: it is home to an impressive selection of discotheques, bars and restaurants. It goes without saying, therefore, that this place will appeal mainly to those who like to party day and night, since the discotheques pump out music (mostly English-language) until the wee hours. Finally, to make sure that its ambiance isn't lacking, the hotel joyfully joins the party by providing its guests with a bar with live music. If Acapulco is synonymous in your mind with non-stop partying, this is the place for you!

Rising straight up into the sky, the 18-story **Fiesta Americana Condesa del Mar (18)** *($$$$; pb, tv, ≡, ≈, ℜ, ☉; La Costera 1220, C.P. 33390, between the Glorieta Diana and the golf club, ☎ 84-28-28, ⇥ 84-18-28, toll-free within Mexico ☎ 91-800-50-450, toll-free from the U.S. and Canada ☎ 1-800-FIESTA-1)* has 500 comfortable rooms decorated in a decent yet uninspiring fashion. As the building stands parallel

to the bay, none of the standard rooms offer a full view of the sea. On the other hand, they do all have a small private balcony (the junior suites have a large terrace). The beautifully maintained common areas are somewhat reminiscent of an office building. Ask for a room in the right wing for a view of the sunset, the left for the sunrise. As in any self-respecting hotel in this category, there are bars, restaurants, shops, a beauty salon and all sorts of other services and facilities on the ground floor. The pool, attractively located overlooking the beach, is unfortunately somewhat modest for an establishment of this size. The hotel was built atop a rocky hillock, making it harder to get to the beach (you have to go down a staircase). As this part of the beach is very crowded (there are a number of bars right on the sand), this hotel is best suited to those who enjoy a perpetually lively atmosphere.

From Playa Condesa to Playa Hornitos

Located 100 metres from the beach, the **Motel Acapulco-Hotel Park Acapulco (29)** *($$; ps, ≡, ≈; La Costera 127, between the Glorieta Diana and Parque Papagayo, Apto 269, ☎ 85-54-37, 85-59-92 or 85-60-72, ≈ 85-54-89)* has 88 simple rooms, most laid out around a tree-shaded garden. In the centre of this garden is an attractive swimming pool, lending the spot a touch of refreshing cool. Some of the rooms have a small balcony with a view of the garden (but no privacy), while others, located on the Plaza Bahía side, give onto an uninteresting side street. The simple wooden furniture gives the place an appealing look. Furthermore, each room has a refrigerator. The noise of the air conditioner is somewhat annoying, however. Safes are available at the reception desk from 9am to 9pm. For its more active guests, the place also has tennis courts, open from 7am to 11pm *(50 to 85 pesos/hour)*.

Located right on the beach, the **Howard Johnson Maralisa (20)** *($$$; ps, ≡, tv, ≈, ℜ; La Costera, C.P. 39670, near Calle Alemania, between the Glorieta Diana and Parque Papagayo, ☎ 85-66-77, ≈ 85-92-28, toll-free from the U.S. and Canada ☎ 1-800-446-4656)* has simple rooms decorated in a spare, unimaginative fashion. They are located in two four-story buildings, only one of which faces the sea. Most do not offer a view of the water, and those that do often lack privacy and peace and quiet, since their balconies face right onto the

hotel's two small pools, a constant source of shrieking and laughter. In the common areas, a sign forbidding guests from bringing any food into their rooms makes the place seem literally uninviting.

Although it is categorized as a hotel, the **Bali-Hai (5)** *($$$; ps, ≡, ≈; La Costera 186, between Parque Papagayo and the Glorieta Diana, ☎ 85-70-45 or 85-66-22, ≈ 85-79-72)* is actually a motel. The rooms, on two levels, are decorated with modest, tasteless furniture. The place has two pools surrounded by palm trees, but there is concrete everywhere and the view is limited to the parking lots in front of the rooms. A safe is available at the front desk from 7am to 11pm. The beach is a five-minute walk away.

Compared to the gigantic Qualton Club Acapulco (see p 82), located nearby, the 12-story **Maris Hotel (28)** *($$$; ps, tv, ≡, ≈, ℜ; La Costera, C.P. 39580, between Parque Papagayo and the Glorieta Diana, ☎ 85-85-43 or 85-84-40, ≈ 85-84-92)* seems pretty modest. Its large rooms are decorated in a slightly kitschy fashion and could use some freshening up, but are pleasant nonetheless. This place has the advantage of being located right on Playa Hornos and offering rooms with a balcony looking out onto the sea. Those on the west side even afford a full view of the bay. On the ground floor, a small swimming pool decorated with a pretty pillar carved with Pre-Columbian motifs embellishes the setting. Another plus is that the relatively small number of rooms (84) makes this a decidedly more convivial place than the neighbouring giants. The Maris is also very popular with Mexican families. Unfortunately, the presence of a drainage pipe near the beach (between the Maris and the Qualton) is hardly reassuring.

The **Paraiso Acapulco (32)** *($$$; pb, ≡, tv, ≈, ℜ; La Costera 163, C.P. 39670, near Parque Papagayo, ☎ 85-55-96, ≈ 82-45-64, toll-free in the U.S. and Canada ☎ 1-800-342-AMIGO)*, which offers all-inclusive packages (see p 44), is a 19-story highrise containing rooms equipped with two big beds each. The decor is somewhat outdated and could really use an overhaul. Each room has a private balcony with a view of the sea or the mountains. The hotel pool, located right in front of the beach, is attractive but too small for the number of guests staying here. Also, as the Paraiso Acapulco has no fewer that 417 rooms, the constant comings and goings of the clientele

do not make for a very relaxing atmosphere. However, those seeking peace and quiet can escape to nearby Parque Papagayo.

The **Club del Sol (9)** *($$$; pb, ≡, tv, K, ≈, ℜ, ☺; La Costera, between Parque Papagayo and the Glorieta Diana, ☎ 85-66-00 or 85-62-64, toll-free from the U.S. and Canada ☎ 1-800-782-3292, toll-free within Mexico ☎ 91-800-09-666)* is a group of connected buildings containing fully equipped studios, each with a kitchenette. In the centre of the complex, surrounded by plants, shrubbery and a few palm trees, are several pools, some of which have a bar. Other amenities include a squash court and a gym. The buildings are located 300 metres from the beach, right near the Costera, in a very commercial area. The place has its own bar/restaurant, discotheque and stores, but you'll have no trouble finding everything you need, as far as food and entertainment are concerned, close by. As this mega-complex has no fewer than 400 studios on several streets, ask to see yours before renting it: some afford a view of the pools, while others give directly onto the streets branching off the Costera or right onto the major artery itself. Whichever you choose, bear in mind that this place is best suited to those who enjoy nonstop action and the company of large families.

The 390-room **Continental Plaza (10)** *($$$ or $$$$ for a studio with kitchenette; pb, tv, ≡, ≈, ℜ; La Costera, just past the Glorieta Diana, immediately west of the Paseo del Farallón, ☎ 84-09-09, ≈ 84-20-81, toll-free within Mexico ☎ 91-800-091-100)* hotel complex has two buildings set right on the beach. The main building, which contains the guest rooms, faces straight onto the sea, while the other, made up mostly of studios, stands perpendicular to the bay, offering only a partial view of the water. Furthermore, a new building is going up opposite the main building, which doesn't bode well for the future. The decor of the common areas, featuring lots of stone and woodwork, is attractive but a bit outmoded. Most of the rooms have a balcony, a travertine bathroom and decent furniture. Still, the whole place could use some smartening up. Surrounded by palm trees and equipped with a bar, the large, inviting pool, complete with a water slide for the kids, is definitely a plus, as is the proximity of the major shopping centres. The hotel's numerous shops, spa, day-care service and

various restaurants and bars will delight visitors who like to have everything close at hand and enjoy a lively atmosphere.

After undergoing a major facelift, the former Ritz Acapulco has reopened with a new look and a new name, the **Qualton Club Acapulco (36)** *($$$$; ps, ≡, tv, ≈, ℜ; La Costera, between the Parque Papagayo and the Glorieta Diana, ☎ 86-82-10, ≈ 86-83-24)*. The owners have also decided to adopt a new approach to welcoming guests: the all-inclusive system (see p 44). The place offers two kinds of rooms: the standard "Junior Suites", located in the north wing, and the larger, more luxurious "Luxes" in the south wing. Nearly all rooms in both categories have a private balcony with a view of the sea. They are tastefully decorated in Santa Fe style, with pretty, earthy colours. Hotel facilities include a large swimming pool, a discotheque, an Italian restaurant, a bar and a big terrace with a buffet restaurant. Plans for an exercise room are also in the works. Though the Qualton Club is located right on attractive Playa Hornos, the nearby presence of a drainage pipe (near the Hotel Maris) is not very pleasant or comforting.

One of the giants of the bay, the **Acapulco Playa Suites (1)** *($$$$; pb, ≈, ≡, tv; La Costera 123, Apto 77, C.P. 39670, facing Playa Hornitos, ☎ 85-80-50, ≈ 85-87-31, toll-free from the U.S. and Canada ☎ 1-800-44-83-55, toll-free within Mexico ☎ 91-800-09-190)* boasts 502 suites in two buildings set face to face on the beach. After seeing the rather cold and institutional-looking lobby, visitors will be surprised by the innovative layout of the rooms. First, there is a room containing two beds, and then a small sunken living room with a private balcony. A large opening affords a view of the living room from the bedroom. Despite a questionable choice of colours, the decor is relatively attractive. All the suites have a sofa-bed, making this place a good choice for people travelling with children *(180 pesos/person extra)*. For a pleasant view, opt for the south tower; the balconies in the north one look out onto the Costera. In addition to enjoying a partial view of the bay and the swimming pool, you'll be able to take in the sunset.

A member of the same chain as the Fiesta Americana (see above), the **Acapulco Plaza (2)** *($$$$; pb, tv, ≡, ≈, ℜ, ☺; La Costera 123, C.P. 39670, between the Glorieta Diana and Parque Papagayo, ☎ 85-90-50 or 69-00-00, ≈ 85-52-85 or 85-54-93, toll-free from the U.S. and Canada*

☎ *1-800-FIESTA-1, toll-free within Mexico* ☎ *91-800-50-450)*
stands out not only for its impressive size (28 stories), but also
its futuristic architecture. The two leaning towers (on the
Costera side), which look as if they tilted toward each other in
an earthquake, are eye-catching and striking. Another unusual
sight is the bar (La Jaula) suspended from the roof of the
building by a long cable. To get there, you have to take a little
bridge from the hotel. In contrast to these novel features, the
decor of the common areas is limited to painted concrete and
worn carpeting, in rather depressing shades of brown and
burgundy. The vast majority of the rooms offer only a partial
view of the bay, but they all have a balcony. There is also a
safe in each room. Amenities include a fun-shaped swimming
pool spanned by little bridges, two whirlpool baths, an exercise
room, a tennis court and several bars and restaurants.

From Playa Hornos to the Zócalo

The **Hotel del Valle (14)** *($; ps, ≡, ⊗, ≈; Gonzálo G. Espinosa
150, right near the Costera, on the east side of Parque
Papagayo, ☎ 85-83-36 or 85-83-88)* is a good choice for those
seeking inexpensive accommodations. The place is simple but
clean, with balconies looking out onto the park and even a
small pool. All this for the modest sum of 150 pesos (170
pesos with air conditioning); what more could you ask?

A member of the Best Western chain, the **De Gante (13)** *($$;
pb, ≡, tv; La Costera 265, near the Fuerte San Diego, ☎ 86-39-
09, 86-21-29 or 86-23-00, ⇒ 86-20-19)* faces directly onto the
noisy Costera. It looks outdated both outside and in, but is
nonetheless decently furnished and offers well-kept rooms.
Furthermore, the double windows in the rooms are a real plus
in this busy area. Located near the Zócalo, with its many
reasonable restaurants, the De Gante is a good option for
travellers on a limited budget. Some of the rooms afford a
direct view of the sea, and the beach is right on the other side
of the Costera. However, you might be taken aback by the sign
declaring that anyone who brings food into the hotel will be
penalized—hardly the most welcoming message!

The sole attraction of **Las Hamacas (24)** *($$ bkfst incl.; ps, ≡,
tv, ≈, ☉; La Costera 239, just east of Fuerte San Diego, right
near Plaza 5 de Mayo, ☎ 83-77-46 or 83-77-09, ⇒ 83-05-75)*,

which is more like a motel than a hotel, is its big pool surrounded by palm trees. The rooms, divided among three stories,
all have their own terrace, but only those on the second and
third floors offer any privacy. Generally speaking, the furniture
is rather worn, and some of the hallways leading to the rooms
are dark and gloomy-looking. For a relatively attractive view (of
the pool and the indoor garden), ask for a room on the top
floor. To get to the beach, 500 metres away, you have to cross
the Costera, which is not always an easy task. Although the
rates are high for what you get, this is still a relative bargain for
travellers on a tight budget.

Though it looks modern from the outside, the six-story **El
Cid (15)** *($$; ps, ≡, ≈, ℜ; La Costera 248, facing Playa Hornos,
between Parque Papagayo and the Zócalo, ☎ 85-13-12, ⌨ 85-
13-87)* has modest rooms. Most have their own balcony, but
these aren't very private, as they face directly onto the hotel's
small pool. The furniture is somewhat outmoded and purely
utilitarian, and the place is practically devoid of decoration. For
an unimpeded view, ask for a top-floor room facing onto the
Costera. A grassy terrace and a handful of palm trees serve to
remind guests that they are in the tropics. The beach is near
by, right on the other side of the Costera.

The Peninsula de las Playas

Despite the depressing presence of an abandoned building just
opposite, the **Hotel Playa Caleta (33)** *($$ with ⊗, with no view,
$$$ with ≡ and view; ps; Calle Alta 19, facing Playa Caleta,
☎ 83-37-24)* deserves a mention for its location, right on Playa
Caleta and just next to Playa Caletilla. The rooms are very
simply decorated but clean. The ones on the beach side are
brighter, making them more inviting. This hotel is very popular
with Mexican tourists. Definitely modest, but cheap!

Perched on a hillock overlooking Playa Caleta, the **Grand
Meigas (19)** *($$$; ps, tv, ≡, ≈, ℜ; Cerro de San Martín, near
Playa Caleta, ☎ 83-93-34 or 83-78-35, ⌨ 83-91-25, toll-free
within Mexico ☎ 91-800-09-200)* uses the all-inclusive system.
The rooms each have their own balcony, and have the added
advantage of offering a clear view of the sea. The modern,
nondescript furnishings are limited to the bare necessities,
making for fairly monotonous surroundings. Still, the brightly

coloured decorative touches here and there, combined with the pretty view from the balcony, help warm the place up. Though the complex is not right on the beach, the sand is only about a hundred metres away, and is easily accessible from the hotel. Also, in the hotel's attractive waterfront garden/terrace, guests can enjoy the use of two large pools, one built at the top of a small cliff.

Would you ever have thought that one day you'd be able to stay in the same room once used by such celebrities as John Wayne, Johnny Weissmuller (Tarzan), Cary Grant, Errol Flynn and scores of other Hollywood stars? Well, this fantasy can become a reality at the **Los Flamingos (25)** *($$$-$$$$ with private terrace; ps, ≡, ≈, ℜ; Lopez Mateos, near Av. Coyuca; this hotel is hard to find, so it is best to get there by taxi; the trip costs about 8 pesos from Playa Caleta; C.P. ☎ 82-06-90, 82-06-91 or 82-06-92, ≈ 83-98-06)*, located on a hillside 10 minutes from Playa Caleta. This hotel, which was built in the 1930s and has preserved all the style of that era, was actually purchased by John Wayne and a number of other actors in 1954. The star's former concierge, Adolfo Santiago, bought the establishment in 1960. Near the front desk, guests can admire a collection of old photographs of the many stars who stayed here over the years. Although the rooms are as modest as can be (motel-style), their location, at the edge of a cliff, with a view out over the sea and Isla Roqueta, lends the place a great deal of charm. Some face onto a common porch, while others have their own balcony. The latter also have air conditioning, which is not quite as necessary up here, thanks to the breeze. Finally, avid John Wayne fans will be pleased to learn that they can rent the *casa redonda* (rate determined by the owner on a case by case basis), a place the actor was particularly fond of. Located a slight distance from the hotel, this small, circular house was the actor's home while in Acapulco. Whichever option you choose, peace and quiet is guaranteed at Los Flamingos, making it particularly well-suited to those wishing to escape the racket of the city. If you'd simply like to visit the premises, it is worth noting that the hotel has a pretty bar, where guests have a unique chance to taste the famous *Coco Loco*, which was supposedly invented here!

From the outside, the **Plaza Las Glorias (35)**, also known as "Le Mirador" *($$$$; pb, ≡, ≈, tv, ℜ; Quebrada 74, Col. La Mira, C.P. 39300, ☎ 83-12-60 or 83-11-55, ≈ 82-45-64)* does not

have a great deal of charm. After passing through the slightly institutional-looking lobby, however, you'll have the pleasure of finding a group of appealing little houses. Some of these are literally clinging to the cliffs, while others are scattered higher up, on a hillside. Most have a private balcony, but only some offer a direct view of the sea. Access to the rooms is gained by a series of trails and staircases that lead through pretty, flower-filled gardens. You might even have to take a cablecar or two to reach your lodgings. The rooms are decorated with tropical accents and the place is well-maintained. Guests enjoy the use of three swimming pools, one filled with salt water. As the place is located right next to the cliffs where the famous *clavadistas* plunge into the water (see p 67), you can take in the show from the big bar/terrace for 61 pesos, which will also buy you two drinks. To reach the Plaza las Glorias from the Zócalo, take Calle La Quebreda, which, after a good uphill stretch, will take you straight to the Plaza Las Glorias.

 RESTAURANTS

In order to make this chapter easier to read, we have used the short form "La Costera", often used by Acapulco residents, to refer to Avenida Miguel Alemán. Also, because the Bay of Acapulco is so long (16 km), we have divided it into five areas (see inside front cover) thus facilitating the task of locating the various restaurants. From east to west, these five areas are **Playa Icacos, Playa Condesa, Playa Condesa to Playa Hornitos, Playa Hornos to the Zócalo** and the **Península de las Playas.**

Playa Icacos

Literally stuck between its competitors, **Checkers** *($; just west of the Days Inn)* is a small, very modest-looking restaurant that is very popular with Mexicans, who come here for the *comida corrida*, a mere 18 pesos. A real bargain in this part of the bay, where everything is more expensive.

At the **Taco Inn** *($; La Costera 22, opposite the Days Inn),* which is decorated in a modern style with little tables topped with colourful ceramic tiles, you can sample as many different kinds of tacos as you can eat. Tasty and cheap, be it midday

or midnight. For insomniacs and night owls, the kitchen is open until 6am on Fridays and Saturdays.

One of a series of restaurants with outdoor seating, **100% Natural** *($; every day 7am to 11pm; west of the Costera, also see p 96)* doesn't look very inviting at first glance. The tables are not the cleanest, and the dishes could certainly be replaced (chipped cups, cracked plates). Nevertheless, there is no denying that few restaurants on this part of the Costera serve as economical and complete a vegetarian breakfast as this place. Judge for yourself: 16 pesos for a meal including juice, a fresh fruit appetizer, yogourt with cereal, two slices of toast with jam and an excellent *café de la olla* (the colloquial term for filter coffee). Those who prefer the traditional egg breakfast will be delighted to find that it comes with whole-wheat bread. Though this place scores low on the aesthetic scale, the quality of the food and the friendly, efficient service make it a good choice.

As indicated by its name, **El Cabrito** *($; every day 2pm to 1am; La Costera 1480, near the Hard Rock Café, ☎ 84-77-11)* specializes in goat dishes. Its curious menu includes stuffed goat's head; supposedly, the eyes are the best part! Goat's-eye-lovers take note! If this kind of food doesn't whet you're appetite, however, you can always opt for the *mole negro oaxaqueño*, a specialty of the State of Oaxaca. This delicious dish consists of Mexican tortillas with the filling of your choice, covered with onions and a thick, chocolate-based sauce, with a sprinkling of Oaxaca cheese on top. A mouthwatering must!

In a country-style setting featuring an open terrace with a ceramic floor, **Fersato's** *($$; La Costera 44, opposite the Casa de la Cultura, ☎ 84-39-49)* serves up *pollo mole* (see p 47) and an excellent *filete al mojo de ajo* (filet of fish with garlic butter), with a salad and real French-fried potatoes on the side. The pickled vegetables served with the bread are excellent. Good value.

Of all the **Sanborn's** *($$; La Costera, near the Days Inn)* on the Costera, the most pleasant is definitely the one in the new Oceanico 2000 shopping centre. Recently opened, it offers an attractive, air-conditioned dining room in spanking-new surroundings. Fans of full-flavoured coffee will be pleased to know that right near by, in the lobby, there is a small stand

that serves real espresso for only 8 pesos. A little farther along the Costera is another **Sanborn's** *($$; La Costera, right before the Costera A Vieja)*. This place used to be a Denny's restaurant, and it's a little depressing, but renovations are planned for the near future. For the moment, there is only a small "bookstore" section and a scant selection of records, as opposed to other, more established Sanborn's. Still, with all the bars and discotheques near by, the place seems bound for better days.

If you are craving Italian food, head straight to the **Spaghetti House** *($$; La Costera 78-2, across from the Calinda Beach hotel)*, where you can take your pick from 16 different pasta dishes, a wide selection of pizza and various Neapolitan specialties. Uninspiring decor.

Los Rancheros *($$; Carretera Escénica 38, near the Extasis discotheque, ☎ 84-19-08)*, which specializes in Mexican cuisine, is known mainly for its *pozole* nights, featuring a transvestite show (every Thursday from 6pm to 10pm). On those evenings, the place is also very popular with gays.

Mariscos Pipos *($$$; every day 1pm to 9:30pm; La Costera, opposite the Centro de Convenciones, west of the Hard Rock Café, ☎ 84-01-65)*, part of a family chain (also see p 96), is reputed among Mexicans for its wide selection of seafood dishes. This location has the advantage of being open later and being located near various services. The plastic plates could definitely go, though.

With its terrace lined with palm trees and decked out with plants and its dining room filled with all sorts of old objects, this **100% Natural** *($$; every day 7am to 11pm; La Costera 34, opposite the Days Inn and the Oceanico 2000 complex)* is the most pleasant member of the chain. Unfortunately, there is no breakfast special, so you have to put together an inexpensive meal on your own. Furthermore, the prices are higher here than at the other locations (see p 96). On the other hand, the portions of food and juice are literally enormous, and two people can easily share (*compartir*) one dish.

Mansión *($$$; La Costera 81, opposite the golf club, ☎ 81-07-96)* is a veritable shrine for carnivores. The grill is as tender as can be, but the side dishes leave something to be

desired. The vegetables aren't varied enough and guests are charged extra for the baked potatoes or fries served with their main dish! It should whet your appetite to learn that you can enjoy a 650-gram Rib Eye Argentino for 115 pesos and an 800-gram *churrasco* for 105 pesos. There are also daily specials starting at 58 pesos. As for the drinks, you may feel inclined toward moderation, given the high prices (14 pesos for a domestic beer!). Despite their grand names, the desserts are disappointing and overpriced (though we recommend the *crepas de cajeta*, a type of caramel tortilla). One last little irritant: the *propina* (tip) is automatically added to the bill. Despite these annoyances, all will be set right once you taste the excellent espresso at the end of your meal. Furthermore, what with the attractive exposed beams, tile floor and pretty, vibrant paintings on the walls, it would be a shame not to enjoy the surroundings—especially since the meat is top-quality.

Located in the Hotel Elcano (see p 76), **Bambuco** *($$$$; La Costera 75, ☎ 84-19-50)* is just the place for visitors looking to spend a quiet evening in a sophisticated setting. On a terrace facing directly onto Playa Icacos, sheltered by little metal roofs made to look like palapas, you can savor a refreshing *gaspacho* followed by *camarones al ajillo*, a delectable *paella valenciana* or a filet of *huachinango*. Comfortably ensconced in a wicker chair, the breeze caressing the nearby palm trees, you can let yourself be lulled by the soft murmurs of the restless waves. Though a bit on the expensive side, this is also an extremely pleasant place to have breakfast (about 40 pesos).

Set up inside a sober-looking villa, the **Suntory** *($$$$; every day 2pm to midnight; La Costera 36, near the Hotel Palapa and the CICI water park , ☎ 84-80-88 or 84-87-66)*, like any self-respecting Japanese restaurant, offers not only sushi, but also *teppan-yaki* tables. Small morsels of fish or meat are cooked right in front of you, then transferred straight to your plate and served with delicious vegetables and rice. The decor, as Japanese as can be, is elegant, but the restaurant's most striking features are its outdoor seating area and the magnificent (we are not exaggerating!) garden in front of it. Anglers will be pleased to learn that they can fish their own meal out of the restaurant's pool. The prices are fairly high, but the service is impeccable.

Heladería *(ice cream shop)*

In a somewhat Americanized decor, **Baskin & Robbins** *(opposite the Sanborn's Oceanico 2000)* has a wide selection of ice cream, including lowfat varieties with no added sugar. Body-conscious visitors take note!

Playa Condesa

If you're looking for a **Sanborn's** (see p 97) near the beach and all the action, the one facing Playa Condesa *($$; La Costera 1226, near the Torres Gemelas)* is a good place to go, especially because it has outdoor seating.

100% Natural *($$; Plaza Acapulco, just west of Carlos 'n Charlie's)*, on the second floor of a big building, has a very attractive decor featuring metal palm trees and lots of plants, with canopies overhead. The only sour note in this elegant setting is the neon lighting. The menu includes copious salads and delicious soy-burgers. As at the other 100% Natural opposite the Days Inn (see p 88), the prices are a little high, but the portions are enormous. Oddly enough, the only credit card accepted here is American Express.

Finding a Chinese restaurant in Acapulco is no easy task. If a craving for Asian cuisine suddenly hits you, head to the **Shangri La** *($$; Piedra Picuda, near the Blue Jeans store, by the Fiesta Americana Condesa hotel, ☎ 84-73-47)*, where you can savour authentic Cantonese cuisine. Don't be put off by the uninviting entrance; the dining area is set in a pleasant inner courtyard, sheltered from the noise of the Costera. The furnishings and decor in general could use some serious touching-up, however. Beneath tall trees, you can tuck into such classic Chinese dishes as duck with almonds, sweet and sour pork, beef with sautéed vegetables, etc. A number of economical two-person meals are also offered. About 55 to 85 pesos per person for three appetizers, three main dishes, dessert and coffee. Excellent value.

Frequented by a young clientele, **Carlos 'n Charlie's** *($$$; La Costera 112, facing Playa Condesa, near the Torres Gemelas, ☎ 84-00-39)* is a place where people go mainly for drinks and a light snack. If you like English-language music played at full

blast, this place will be right up your alley. As far as the decor is concerned, eccentricity is definitely the watchword here. Up on the second floor, all sorts of paraphernalia, ranging from giant baseball caps attached to the ceiling to an immense hanging megaphone, which the waiter uses to yell out his order, set the tone. In a small loggia on the same floor, a baker makes the buns served with the food. At the sound of the bell (another creative touch, but also a necessity, given the noise level!), the bread is delivered to the waiters in a wicker basket lowered with a rope. In short, if you're looking for peace and quiet, steer clear of this place. Good Mexican and international food. Fun and moderately expensive.

Surrounded by a bunch of tacky-looking bars, **Beto** *($$$; La Costera, facing Playa Condesa, near the Safari and Black Beards,* ☎ *84-04-73)* is an inviting place, located below the Costera, facing the beach. After walking down a series of stairs adorned with scores of plants, you'll find yourself in front of a pretty, equally verdant outdoor seating area. Here in this exotic setting, seated at an attractive table sheltered by palm trees, you can enjoy a candlelight meal of tasty shrimp or, if you prefer meat, a tender filet mignon. Though it is located in a particularly noisy and touristy area and its prices are a bit high, this place deserves a mention for its relatively quiet atmosphere and elegant decor.

For Italian cuisine in a sophisticated setting, head to **Raffaello** *($$$; La Costera 1221,* ☎ *84-01-00)*, near the Torres Gemelas. For a refreshing start to your meal, try the *ensalada salsa roquefort* (salad with roquefort sauce) or the *ensalada caprese* (unfortunately, it contains cheddar cheese rather than bocconcini). Next, the spaghetti *armando*, with tuna and peas, and the osso buco are sure bets for your main course. Finally, for a sweet finale, the strawberry and apricot pies are both recommended. The main dining room, with its high ceilings and pretty stone pillars, is decorated with earthenware jars set off by lights, as well as lots of plants. A very elegant entrance, adorned on either side by stained-glass windows showing various parts of Italy, enhances the decor. The service is impeccable, if a bit overattentive.

At first sight, **El Campanario** *($$$$; every day 6pm to midnight; on a hillside above the Panoramic hotel; take Calle del Morro then the first right and follow the signs,* ☎ *84-88-30 or*

84-88-31), set on a large piece of property, looks like a converted monastery. However, though it looks old and is graced with a little bell tower, it actually only dates from 1985 and most certainly has never served any religious purpose. Built high upon a hillside, this restaurant offers a breathtaking view of the entire bay from its wide terrace. After passing through its majestic entryway, visitors will discover a series of small, vaulted rooms with handsome brick columns. The rustic furniture and lovely wood and leather chairs around the tables lend the place a bit of a colonial air. The giant earthenware jars set here and there and the scores of plants hanging in wicker baskets serve as pretty finishing touches to the decor. The cuisine, for its part, is good, but the enchanting setting might lead one to hope for a bit more creativity. All in all, though, the menu is quite extensive, and given the unique surroundings, it would be a shame not to come here at least once, if only to take in the view over drinks. This place is hard to get to, so it is best to take a taxi *(it should cost you no more than 20 pesos from the Costera).* Reservations recommended.

It doesn't take much guesswork to figure out what sort of cuisine is featured at **La Petite Belgique-Aux Moules Belges** *($$$$-$$$$$; in the centre of Plaza Marbella, right by the Glorieta Diana,* ☎ *84-77-25 or 84-20-17).* Rabbit with beer, *carbonnades flamandes, chicons au gratin,* "moules-frites" (mussels and fries) and all sorts of other typical Belgian dishes are served here, along with those famous beers that only the Belgians seem to be able to make. Guests have the choice between two dining rooms: the first, a partially open terrace, is located near the beach. Unfortunately, though the decor is attractive and the atmosphere relaxed, an unsightly parking lot spoils the view and the overall setting a bit. The second, more sophisticated dining area is located right in the middle of the Plaza, in a small, air-conditioned building. Each place has its own menu, and, like the decor, one is more elaborate (and expensive) than the other. Both menus are available in either restaurant, however. Pricey, but oh! that Belgian cuisine!

From Playa Condesa to Playa Hornitos

The **Restaurante Los Metates** *($; at the corner of Vicente Yañez Pinzón, west of the Glorieta Diana, opposite the Continental Plaza hotel)* has much the same menu and decor as its

neighbour, El Fogón (see below), though some dishes are slightly more expensive here. The fruit plate is a real treat for breakfast, and the *mollete* (a large piece of bread with the crusts removed, covered with *frijoles* and cheese and then baked in the oven) is a hearty, inexpensive meal. An advertisement claims that the restaurant serves the *"el mejor café de Acapulco"* (the best coffee in Acapulco), but we beg to differ!

El Fogón *($$; La Costera, at the corner of Vicente Yañez Pinzón, just past the Glorieta Diana, west of Paseo del Farallón, facing the Continental Plaza hotel)*. This chain of restaurants, very popular with Mexicans, owes its reputation not only to its Mexican cuisine, but also to its famous *molcajete acapulqueño*. The decor of its big terrace, which opens right onto the Costera, consists mainly of wooden tables and red place mats. Excellent value for the money. There's an identical El Fogón a little north, on the same side of the Costera, and another across from the university *(at the corner of Calle C. Gonzalo de Sandoval)*. In terms of both size and decor, however, the latter is the least inviting of the chain.

Vips *($$; across from the Paraiso hotel in the Gran Plaza Acapulco shopping centre, at the corner of Av. Wilfrido Massieu)* falls in the same category as the Sanborn's restaurants (see p 97), but has less charm and higher prices than its competitor. On the other hand, it is open 24 hours a day, an advantage not to be sneered at on this part of the Costera, where few restaurants offer round-the-clock service. This place is therefore particularly practical for breakfast or a late-night snack.

Though the service is a bit slow, it is worth going to the **Sirocco** *($$$; every day 1:30pm to midnight; La Costera, near the Bodega shopping centre, west of Parque Papagayo, on the beach, ☎ 85-23-86 or 85-94-90)* just for the paellas. In addition to authentic *tortillas españolas*, guests of this establishment can sample delicious *tapas* on an elegant beachside terrace.

Heladería *(ice cream shop)*

Santa Clara *(three locations on the Costera: Plaza la Cita, at Calle Alemania, facing the Gran Plaza; in the Galería Acapulco Plaza, and opposite the Oceanica 2000 complex)*. This chain

specializes in ice cream but also serves lowfat frozen yogourt and various flavours of cheese ice cream. The tamarind ice cream is a truly delicious, refreshing treat. The shops are decorated in modern style, and have a small outdoor seating area. Oddly enough, despite a sign indicating the contrary, no coffee is served here!

From Playa Hornos to the Zócalo

Breakfasting in **Parque Papagayo** to the sounds of the numerous birds that make their home here can be a pleasant experience. There are several stands in the park that serve breakfast for as little as 10 pesos. The only drawback is that they don't open until 10am, though you are free to go in Parque Papagayo as early as 6am. Opt for the stand in the northwest end of the park, since it has several tables and is located in a relatively quiet spot.

Located in the heart of the old city, the **Cafetería Astoria** *($; Plaza Alvarez, on the Zócalo to the right of the cathedral)* is nothing but an ordinary cafe, but its location makes it a particularly pleasant place to have a snack. From its outdoor seating area, sheltered by a stately tree, you can observe the nonstop activity on the Zócalo while enjoying a cup of coffee, a Mexican-style sandwich, one of the daily specials or simply some ice cream. The cafe seems to be a very popular meeting place for Mexicans, so you'll find a lot of locals here.

The bar/restaurant **Bocana Beach** *($; every day 9am to 2am; at the west end of Parque Papagayo, at the foot of the cableway, facing the beach, ☎ 85-09-41)* presents *música en vivo* every day of the week from 4pm on, and hosts a *pozole* evening, featuring a transvestite show, every Thursday. You can eat a good, unpretentious meal here for a nominal sum (*comida corrida* for 18 pesos) or simply have a glass of *Coco Frío* (5 pesos). The place also serves breakfast for as little as 12 pesos. Mexican atmosphere guaranteed.

The **Restaurante Balneario Hornitos La Cabaña de Perico** *($; La Costera, opposite the Pemex gas station, between Parque Papagayo and the Fuerte San Diego)* is a pleasant place for a good, simple meal. Beneath a palm-frond roof, you can savour seafood and fish dishes in the cool ocean breeze. The proximity

of the beach, lit up in places at night, makes the setting that much more appealing. Full meals starting at 40 pesos.

Among the inexpensive restaurants, **Las Canastas** *($; every day around the clock; La Costera 223, from the Zócalo, turn left on the Costera, heading toward the Fuerte San Diego; across from the Aduana, ☎ 83-87-00)* can hold its head high for the quality of its service. In an inviting setting featuring pretty carved-wood chairs and lots of hanging plants, you'll be served the *comida corrida* or some *chili con carne* for as little as 12 pesos. A two-person seafood meal is also available for 90 pesos; meat lovers only have to spend 50 pesos. A breakfast of *huevos divorciados* only costs 13 pesos. A real bargain! The only sour note is the television in the dining room. Good value.

A little farther south, **Las Parillas** *($$; La Costera, near the entrance of the Fuerte San Diego)* hosts a *pozole* night every Thursday for 77 pesos. On the ground floor, the decor is very attractive, with lovely brick arches, handsome old wooden chairs and pretty, colourful tablecloths. The second-floor dining room is not as charming, but has a dance floor. The menu is standard, the food good but simple.

Set right on the beach, with a big roof covered with palm fronds, the **Copacabana** *($$; noon to 3am; on the beach side of the Costera, just east of Av. D. Mendoza)* serves Mexican dishes in an exotic setting with a hot, very Latin ambiance. Thursday is *pozole* night, complete with a show. Very popular with Mexicans.

Just below the Costera, on a small quay, the **Restaurante-Bar Colonial** *($$; La Costera 130, at the Club de Playa Acapulco, right before the Fuerte San Diego, ☎ 83-91-07)* is a very modest-looking place. With its nearly absent decor, corrugated iron roof and blue lighting at night, it is nonetheless one of the most romantic spots around. Seated at one of its simple tables, you can enjoy a superb view of the bay and admire the myriad twinkling lights that bring it to life at night. The *margaritas* are served according to Mexican tradition (also see p 50), and the house specialties, seafood and fish, are worth the trip. The cold *mariscos* appetizer, a delicious blend of shrimp, sea snails and squid, is sure to win many a fan. After your meal, if you feel like it, you can even dance a bit on the quay to authentic Mexican music.

On your way up and down the Costera, you'll spot a number of restaurants called **100% Natural**. These places serve salads, yogourt, fresh fruit, soyburgers and all sort of other vegetarian foods. However, upon closer inspection, you'll see that the menus vary considerably from one place to the next, and that the decor ranges from terrific to terrible. Unfortunately, the same can also be said of the food, and travellers will probably make the surprising discovery that the coffee is flavourless at one place and excellent in another bearing the same name and located just a short distance away. As a general rule, those with the palm-tree logo instead of the percentage sign (%) have a more attractive and more sophisticated decor. However, they are also more expensive, and, unlike the others, don't offer an inexpensive breakfast special. The only constant is that the servings are always gigantic. If you feel like it (or rather if your stomach does!), ask to share a dish. To help you find your way in this "palm-tree jungle", we have listed a few locations that stand out for their pleasant decor, quality food or excellent service (see p 87, p 88, p 90 and below).

100% Natural *($$; La Costera, right by the El Cid hotel, facing Playa Hornos, between Parque Papagayo and the Zócalo).* Despite its modest appearance, this restaurant deserves a mention for its attractive decor and its location, in an area where there aren't many places to eat early in the morning. Unfortunately, there is no breakfast special.

Reputed for their vast selection of seafood dishes, the **Mariscos Pipos** *($$; every day noon to 8pm; Almirante Breton 9, a few streets west of the Zócalo, just past the old port, ☎ 82-22-37 or 83-88-01, also see p 88)* restaurants serve octopus, fish, shrimp, shellfish, sea snails and all sorts of other little sea creatures. Over the years, the Pipos family has grown considerably and now has no fewer than four restaurants (two in the bay, one in Puerto Marqués and another near the airport). The general layout, identical at all four locations, consists of a large, somewhat cold-looking terrace warmed up by small, bright yellow tablecloths and a few small pieces of wooden furniture. As far as the food is concerned, it can only be described as average. For your appetizer, you're better off with the *ceviche* than the shrimp cocktail, which is accompanied by an uninspired sauce.

Anyone who already knows Mexico is probably no stranger to **Sanborn's** *($$)*, a country-wide chain with four locations along the Costera. These places are reputed both for the quality of their food and for their quick, efficient service. The menu consists mainly of Mexican cuisine, with a few international dishes thrown in. Hearty and delicious breakfasts are also served up here. Furthermore, the various Sanborn's are among the few places in the bay to offer espresso (at the slightly exorbitant price of 12 pesos, however). Attached to each restaurant is a shop selling books, records, cosmetics, etc. Though most Sanborn's have a similar decor, in Acapulco, some are more attractive than others. The one in the old city, near the Zócalo, is singularly devoid of charm and somewhat depressing, despite its impeccable service (also see p 87, 90).

Heladería *(ice cream shop)*

Depite its nonexistent decor and somewhat depressing terrace, **Teposnieve** *(La Costera, right near the Centro Acapulco port, not far from the Fuerte San Diego)* is noteworthy for its large choice of ice cream and exceptionally low prices.

The Península de las Playas

To the right of the Hotel Playa Caleta (see p 84), right on the beach, you'll find a multitude of little restaurants, pretty much all of which offer an identical menu made up chiefly of inexpensive fish and seafood dishes *(15 to 30 pesos)*. Full breakfasts are also served here for as little as 17 pesos.

The **Restaurante La Cabaña de la Caleta** *($; left of the Hotel Playa Caleta)*, whose pleasant location sets it apart from its numerous competitors, deserves a mention for its lovely beachside terrace. The ingredients of its charm: flowers all around and small tables with placemats and pretty settings. The cuisine, standard but good, consists mainly of seafood dishes and meat brochettes. Both drinks and food are reasonably priced.

ENTERTAINMENT

Nearly all the big hotels on the Costera have their own night-spots. Take a stroll along Playa La Condesa, one of the local meccas for night owls, where you'll have no trouble finding a bar or discotheque to your liking. Keep in mind that many places have cover charges and strict dress codes (no shorts for men). These factors vary not only according to the season, but also the day, with the cover as much as tripling. In some cases, this charge entitles the guest to a drink or access to an "open bar"—that is, "free" domestic drinks for part of the evening.

In order to make this chapter easier to read, we have used the short form "La Costera", often used by Acapulco residents, to refer to Avenida Miguel Alemán. Also, because the Bay of Acapulco is so long (16 km), we have divided it into five areas (see inside front cover), thus facilitating the task of locating the various bars and restaurants. From east to west, these five areas are **Playa Icacos**, **Playa Condesa**, **Playa Condesa to Playa Hornitos**, **Playa Hornos to the Zócalo**, and the **Península de las Playas**.

Playa Icacos

Globe-trotting rock 'n' rollers will be happy to learn that they won't feel too much like fish out of water in this part of the world, thanks to the local **Hard Rock Café** (La Costera, near the CICI water park, ☎ 84-66-80). There's no point describing the decor, as the Hard Rock formula is adhered to just as strictly here as anywhere else. Fans of this British chain will nonethe-less be surprised to see that the horrible rotating sign is just one more factor that detracts from the appearance of the area, which has already been considerably disfigured! High prices.

Right next to the Hard Rock Café, you'll find its American "cousin", **Planet Hollywood** (La Costera, near the CICI water park, ☎ 84-00-47). All of Hollywood awaits you here, and seeing as everything is supposed to be bigger in America, it is in a huge globe held by two giant hands that guests enter the realm of the imaginary. Seated at a table or leaning on the bar, you can thus escape among the Hollywood stars. However,

your trip to the city of dreams ends with a rather steep bill. Whoever said it doesn't hurt to dream! As at the Hard Rock Café, you can add to your collection of t-shirts, baseball caps, pins, etc. before you leave—and even pay for your purchases in U.S. dollars. Oh! Beautiful Acapulco, where has your Mexican spirit gone? Fun? Shameful? Sophisticated? Stupefying? You can decide for yourself.

The discotheque **Baby'O** *(La Costera 22, near Yucatán, opposite the Days Inn, near the restaurant Suntory)* has the reputation of being very selective, so don't even think of showing up in shorts! After making it through its carefully guarded entrance (phew!), you can kick up your heels to the latest hits. A note to those who like to go to bed early: on Saturday nights, the crowd keeps rolling in until 6am!

Judging from its exterior, you might conclude that the **Disco Ninas** *(cover charge; La Costera, a little west of the Hard Rock Café and Planet Hollywood)* is a cheap replica of Planet Hollywood! Rest assured: it is nothing of the sort, but rather a hopping discotheque where you can dance to Latin American and English-language music. Though the atmosphere is a bit uptight, this is a pleasant place to spend an evening.

Those looking for more authentic Mexican entertainment should take note that a variety of folk shows are presented several times a week in the bay. The following is one of the best:

At the Centro Cultural y de Convenciones de Acapulco *(La Costera, next to the golf club, Playa Icacos)*, you can attend the **Fiesta Mexicana**, organized by the Folk Ballet of the City of Acapulco. For over three hours, spectators get to watch regional dances and listen to traditional music not only from the State of Guerrero, but also from the neighbouring States of Jalisco, Michoacán and Chiapas. As a bonus, you get to take in the spine-tingling spectacle of the Papantla Voladores, acrobats who perform stunts around a pole to which they are attached. The evening will cost you about US$50, including a meal and three hours of entertainment. The show is only presented three times a week *(Mon, Wed and Fri 7pm to 10pm, ☎ 84-72-04, ext. 448, or 84-32-18)* during the high season, so reservations are strongly recommended. Touristy but lots of fun.

Playa Condesa

Just west of the Fiesta Americana hotel (see p 78), you'll find an impressive string of bars and discotheques interspersed with all different kinds of restaurants and snack bars. This area is commonly known as Disco Beach. It all starts with the **Safari**, decorated entirely with wood, next come **Beto** and its pretty, exotic-looking terrace, **Black Beards**, **Barba Roja**, whose terrace is designed to look like the upper deck of a pirate ship, and the spotlessly white **Paradise**, then ends a little farther with the **Taboo**. The action heats up slowly, starting at 5pm; reaches its peak around midnight and stays at that level until 2am, when the crowds start migrating to the big discotheques in the bay. Some places have outdoor seating right on the beach, while others are located alongside the Costera, with a view of the sea. They are all trying to outdo each other, and most seem to be trying to attract passing tourists by making their decor as original as possible. Nevertheless, they all play the same kind of music, namely, the same tunes that can be heard in big discotheques all over the world. The only exception is the Taboo, which seems more fond than the others of Latin music. In general, these places will appeal chiefly to people who like to mingle with other tourists. Despite their lack of local colour, however, they have the advantage of serving reasonably priced drinks. Furthermore, most don't have any cover charge.

From Playa Condesa to Playa Hornitos

Located at the end of the street opposite the Continental Plaza hotel, the **Prince** *(30 pesos Fri and Sat, 20 pesos Sun to Thu; behind the restaurant El Fogón)* is the last stop on young revelers' tours of the bay's bars and discotheques. This place is enjoying greater and greater popularity with a widely varied clientele including youths, couples, gays, heterosexuals, students and businessmen, most of whom are Mexican. The secret of its success: domestic drinks at low prices (five beers served in an ice bucket for 30 pesos, hard alcohol for 10 pesos) and an exceptionally wide range of music covering all different tastes. For those who get here early, shows are presented at midnight. The Prince has a single, big room split up into various levels, each with tables, sofas and a small space for dancing;

at the foot of these various "steps" is a large dance floor. There is a lineup on weekends, so be prepared to be patient. After all, the night has just begun! A true after-hours club, the Prince doesn't close until 1pm!

From Playa Hornos to the Zócalo

The **Disco Iguanas Ranas** *(80 pesos from 10pm to 4:30am; opposite the Bodega supermarket)*, one of the various places using the "open bar" system, is set right on the beach and has a *palapa* roof. Despite its exotic name, it plays English-language music for the most part, ranging from rap to rock and disco. The dance floor is fairly small, given the number of tables. As is usual in Acapulco tradition, the atmosphere doesn't really pick up until midnight, and the liveliest nights are Friday, Saturday and Sunday. If the place isn't crowded, there is no cover charge, but rather a minimum purchase of one domestic drink (15 pesos).

Those who like tropical evenings will probably have more fun at the **Tropicana** *(10 pesos; every day 9:30pm to 4:30am; on the beach side of the Costera, south of Av. D. Mendoza, before the Iguanas Ranas)* than at any of the other discotheques on the Costera. From Tuesday to Sunday, live musicians play here until the wee hours, electrifying a crowd of writhing dancers. The music, almost exclusively Latin, is very enjoyable, and the decor, topped by a *palapa* roof, as exotic as can be. Even if you don't plan on dancing, the odds are high that after one of the potent house margaritas (15 pesos for domestic drinks), you, too, will kick up your heels. Don't worry: everyone has fun here – young and old, couples and singles. As an added bonus, you can admire the surrounding beach, all lit up, and the bay twinkling off in the distance.

Gay Bars and Discotheques

Although Acapulco attracts large numbers of gay visitors, there are surprisingly few gay nightspots here. A few of the bars along the Costera, being very popular with tourists, naturally attract a certain number of gay customers, but do not cater exclusively to homosexuals. These are described earlier in the

"Entertainment" section. Below, we have listed the places that declare themselves to be gay, even if they are open to all. For the most part, these are discotheques; during daytime, the most popular gay hangout is Playa Condesa (see p 69), just west of the Fiesta Americana Condesa (see p 78).

Disco Demas *(30 pesos including one domestic drink; Costera A. Vieja, the street right before the restaurant Carlos 'n Charlie's, near the Torres Gemelas)*, which also attracts women and a few heterosexual men, is frequented mainly by a young crowd (18 to 30). The music is English-language, with some more Latin rhythms thrown in here and there. Transvestite shows are presented on the weekend, and there are strippers "strolling" along the counter at all times. The drinks are moderately priced (15 to 20 pesos for a domestic drink), and the waiters may encourage you to toss back as many as possible.

Frequented by Mexicans of all ages, the **Relax** *(30 pesos including one drink; on the little street right before Costera A. Vieja, right by the Sanborn's...)* is arguably the best gay discotheque in Acapulco. The friendly, unpretentious atmosphere starts livening up at midnight and doesn't wind down until daybreak! An excellent show featuring transvestites and nude dancers is presented from 1:30am to 2am. You're sure to appreciate the *Reina del show* and his imitation of singer Chelo Silva. The music, both Mexican and English-language, is varied enough to satisfy most tastes. Not to be missed!

If you really enjoy watching nude dancers and are ready to pay the price to do so, the **Malinche** *(on the little street behind the Galería Plaza Acapulco shopping centre)* will be right up your alley. It should be noted, however, that the business practices of this place are not always as honest as they might be, and that there is a special price for every drink purchased for the dancers or "other clients".

 SHOPPING

While some people consider Acapulco the "pearl of the Pacific", it can also take pride in being a veritable paradise for shopaholics. An infinite (the word is hardly an exaggeration!) number of boutiques stretch along the bay, and the only

problem you'll have is settling on what to buy. Clothing, leather goods, jewellery, crafts and all sorts of other objects are displayed in one shop window after another. If you're looking to take home a little souvenir, here are some suggestions:

While exploring the bay, you will probably notice that there are a large number of flourishing *mercados artisanales* all along the Costera. Most of these sell the same merchandise. Be prepared to face a crowd of vendors vaunting their merchandise (in English) as you approach. Also, take note that in this "den" of consumerism it is literally impossible to shop without being bothered by salespeople. If this image doesn't scare you off and you have gifts to buy, relax, put a smile on your face and above all, feel free to bargain, since the craftspeople are not selling their products here directly, and the employees are used to haggling. **El Parazal Mercado** and the **Artesenía del Centro** *(right beside the Commercial Mexicana store)* are two of the crafts markets for tourists along the Costera. On the same noisy artery, farther west, the **Mercado de Artesanía** *(facing Plaza Marbella)* is a similar market. Finally, facing Plaza Bahía, the **Mercado de Artesanías El Pueblito** and the **Mercado de Artesanías Dalia** *(next to the Acapulco Plaza)* sell the same types of products.

If you are looking for someplace more fun, however, head to the market alongside **Parque Papagayo**, along Playa Hornitos. Though the merchandise here is also very touristy and not always tasteful, the atmosphere is more appealing, since the market is frequented chiefly by Mexican travellers. Finally, a word of advice for die-hard shoppers: no matter what you're

looking for, always remember these three rules: be patient, negotiate, and compare.

It would be a real shame to leave Mexico without some sort of musical souvenir. If you aren't convinced, stop by one of the two **Jazzz** *(La Costera 125, in the Plaza Bahía shopping centre and Av. Cuauhtémoc 15, near the Zócalo)* stores. *Mariachi* music doesn't appeal to you? No matter! Ask to hear famous singers Selena and Viki Carr, or a *ranchero* band, and you're sure to be impressed by the infinite variety of Mexican song. If you still haven't been won over, a salesperson can always dig up one of those boisterous salsas or perhaps an Abba or Nana Mouskouri tune sung in Spanish!

On the Gran Plaza Acapulco *(La Costera and Av. Wilfrido Massieu)*, you'll find the **Salinas y Rochas** department store, known all over Mexico. While the store is hardly unique and could be compared to department stores in Paris, Montreal or Chicago, if you look around a little (wherever the sales are, of course!), you'll find all sorts of quality products at unbeatable prices. The clothing and shoes are the best bargains.

If you like home furnishings and decorations, make sure to stop by **Lorea Decoración** *(Mon to Fri 10am to 2pm and 4:30pm to 7pm, Plaza Icacos, just north of the Hyatt)*, which sells designer furniture, unusual fabrics, pottery and all sorts of other items.

The little shop **Capricho's** *(La Costera 121-C, ☎ 84-09-09)*, on the ground floor of the Continental Plaza (see p 81), stands out for its lovely selection of pottery from Tlaquepaque. It also sells jewellery, as well as beautiful handcrafted items from various parts of Mexico.

For something out of the ordinary, head to **Sergio Bustamante** *(La Costera 120)*, reputed among artists for its original creations and bizarre figurines (people with two sets of eyes, a sun with a human face, a snail with a man's head, etc.). Beautiful but expensive!

If you are fond of porcelain, make sure to go have a look at **Emilia Castillo**'s *(Carretera Escénica, near the luxurious Las Brisas hotel, on the right side of the road as you head to Puerto Marqués)* creations. This shop, located next to the entrance of

the Madeiras restaurant (see p 115), sells magnificent porcelain objects, as well as sculptures and silver articles. A worthy descendant of Antonio Castillo, an apprentice of the renowned William Spratling (also see p 122), she developed a technique that made it possible to inlay porcelain with silver patterns, with absolutely magnificent, uncommon results. Not to be missed!

You can't leave Acapulco without paying at least one visit to its famous **Mercado Municipal** *(right by Av. Diego Hurtado Mendoza, between Av. Cuauhtémoc and Av. Aquiles Serdán)*, north of the Zócalo. For those who like mingling with the crowd or simply bargain hunting, this large market is, in and of itself, a veritable kaleidoscope of Mexican society. Keep your eyes wide open, as all the colours of the rainbow come together here in the form of fruits, vegetables, spices and all sorts of other foodstuffs. Good taste and bad amicably share space here in an ever-moving crowd, where the cries of salespersons and children blend into one. Among the marvellous sights to behold are countless peppers in all different shapes, luscious green tomatoes, curious medicinal herbs, intriguing *moles* (see p 47) served by the ladle-full and bizarre-looking giant *chicharrones* (fried pork rinds), to name but a few. In the middle of the market, there is a "dining" section where you can sample all sorts of dishes for a few pesos.

Finally, under the heading "health", there's **Super Soya** *(every day 8am to 9pm, Jesús Carranza 9, Col. Centro, near the Zócalo, ☎ 83-55-54)*, where visitors craving organic products will find a large choice of cereal, and can even enjoy a tasty yogourt with some delicious cereal or a good fruit juice.

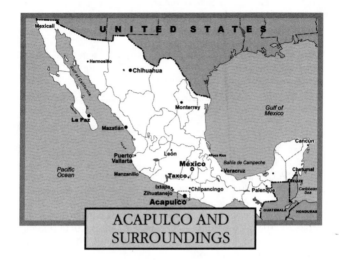

ACAPULCO AND SURROUNDINGS

P ie de la Cuesta, Laguna de Coyuca, Bahía Marqués, so many dreamy names... Located close to the city of Acapulco, these tourist towns make good day-trip destinations. As they are set on either side of the Bay of Acapulco, this chapter divides them into two tours: **Tour A: Bahía Marqués and Environs**, and **Tour B: Pie de la Cuesta**. Each tour may easily be accomplished in one day.

FINDING YOUR WAY AROUND

Tour A: Bahía Marqués and Environs

By Car

From the Bay of Acapulco, take the Costera in the direction of the airport. Then, just after hurtling down the southeast point of the bay, at the first *glorieta*, follow the signs for Bahía Marqués. Playa Revolcadero is situated about seven kilometres from there and may be reached by taking any road on the left side of Carretera Escénica.

By Bus

From the Costera, take any of the many buses marked *Bahía Marqués* (they pass every 15 minutes). The fare is only two pesos and the trip is about half an hour.

Tour B: Pie de la Cuesta

By Car

From the Costera, proceed in the direction of the Zócalo, and, a little past Fuerte San Diego, take Avenida Escudero, which later turns into Avenida Aquiles Serdán, on the right. The road that leads to Pie de la Cuesta is on the left side of the main artery, a little past the intersection with Avenida Cuauhtémoc. The beach and Laguna de Coyuca are situated about 15 kilometres from that point.

By Bus

From the Costera, take any of the many buses marked *Pie de la Cuesta* (also see p 110). The approximately one-hour bus trip costs two pesos.

 EXPLORING

Tour A: Bahía Marqués and Environs

The first attraction along the airport road is none other than **Playa Revolcadero ★**, an immense, fine-sand beach. Relatively deserted, it is the domain of impressive waves and powerful ocean currents that make it foremost a preserve of expert surfers. Swimmers and novice surfers should avoid venturing into the ocean here. Despite this disadvantage, the length of the beach is perfect for long strolls and horses may also be rented here (see p 110). The beauty of this spot, enhanced by the magnificent Acapulco Princess hotel (see p 112), makes it a wonderful stop-off, and nearby **Laguna Tres Palos** can be the

The Hotels
3. Acapulco Princess
7. Casa Blanca
31. Parador del Sol
34. Playa Leonor
39. Ukae Kim

Acapulco and Surroundings

object of nature excursions of particular interest to ornithologists.

More exotic and with richer flora than its "big sister", and still relatively undeveloped, **Bahía Marqués** (also called Bahía de Puerto Marqués) offers beautiful crystalline waters. Once quiet, these waters now attract hordes of swimmers every weekend, and, unless people-watching appeals, they are best avoided on Saturdays and Sundays. Over the last few years, unfortunately, a veritable canopy of beach umbrellas has sprung up, literally obstructing the natural beauty of this spot.

Carretera Escénica ★★ is the main road that leads from the airport to the eastern "gateway" of the Bay of Acapulco. As its Spanish name suggests, this road is dotted with wonderful lookouts over Bahía Marqués, the Bay of Acapulco and the surrounding mountains. Heading toward the city, on the mountaintop which is also home to the Las Brisas hotel

complex (see p 112), is **Capilla de la Paz**. While the area itself is not particularly attractive, and despite the encroachment of houses that seem to be taking the mountainside by storm, this spot is especially enchanting to admirers of magnificent sunsets, and, for early birds, sunrises. This is the highest vantage point over the bay.

Tour B: Pie de la Cuesta

Northwest of Acapulco, about 15 kilometres from the bay on the Zihuatanejo road, is a lovely beach: **Pie de la Cuesta ★**. Very long and shaded by the odd coconut palm, the beach is bordered by a long road that runs between Laguna Coyuca and the Pacific Ocean. Touristic development is still relatively small-scale here, and the area is perfect for solitary strollers and horseback riders seeking vast, unspoiled stretches. This beach is also famous for spectacular sunsets and wild waters, excellent terrain for surfing pros. Swimming is emphatically discouraged because of dangerously strong currents.

Just next to the beach, **Laguna de Coyuca ★**, of similarly impressive dimensions, is an ideal spot for motorized water sports (see p 111). Also, many nature excursions depart from here.

 OUTDOOR ACTIVITIES

 Horseback Riding

Tour A: Bahía Marqués and Environs

At Playa Revolcadero, horses may be rented at the **Acapulco Princess** hotel, where riders can meander the beach. Mexicans offer horse rental at markedly more affordable prices.

Tour B: Pie de la Cuesta

On the beach at Pie de la Cuesta, Mexicans offer horse rental at particularly reasonable rates. Budget for about 70 pesos for

one half-hour of horseback riding. Those wishing to ride for several hours should not hesitate to negotiate a price.

 Golf

Tour A: Bahía Marqués and Environs

An integral part of the luxurious Acapulco Princess hotel, **Golf Club Acapulco Princess** *(Playa Revolcadero,* ☎ *69-10-00 or toll-free in the U.S. and Canada 1-800-223-1818,* ⇆ *69-10-16)* offers an 18-hole golf course in an especially lush and calm environment. The price is 120 pesos, or 75 pesos for hotel guests.

 Water-skiing

Tour B: Pie de la Cuesta

There are many waterskiing equipment outfitters along the main street between the ocean and the lagoon. Among these, **Restaurante Tres Marias** *(on the right side of the street heading west)* has particularly affordable rates. Budget for about 200 pesos per hour.

 Jet-skiing

Tour B: Pie de la Cuesta

Laguna Coyuca boasts relatively unspoiled nature and open spaces away from the throngs of tourists. Plan for 300 pesos per hour for jetski rental at **Restaurante Tres Marias** *(on the right side of the street heading west).*

 Surfing

The most impressive surfing waves break at Playa Revolcadero and at Pie de la Cuesta. Be aware that these two sites are equally renown for their particularly treacherous currents. Surfing in these areas is above all restricted to professionals.

ACCOMMODATIONS

Tour A: Bahía Marqués and Environs

Part of the Westin Hotels & Resorts chain, the heavenly hotel **Las Brisas** *($$$$$ and more..., bkfst incl.; pb, ≡, ≈, K, ℜ; Carretera Escénica, C.P. 39868, ☎ 84-15-80 or toll free in the U.S. and Canada 1-800-223-6800, in Mexico 91-800-90-223, ≠ 84-60-71)* is a vast complex spread over many hectares of hilly terrain at the eastern tip of the bay. No fewer than 261 *casitas* (little cottages) are set on either side of the mountain, half with a view over the Bay of Acapulco, half facing Bahía Marqués. Each cottage has a separate entrance, a large balcony and even a private pool (except for basic units that include one pool per two units). Breakfast is served to guests' rooms every morning. Depending on the location of the room, guests are treated to the sunrise over romantic Bahía Marqués or the sunset over Acapulco as it makes way for the thousand lights that illuminate the bay at night. It goes without saying that the rooms are perfectly equipped and tastefully decorated. Stone predominates as the material for floors and walls, while the pastel colour scheme evokes the fifties without being kitsch. Among the services available are a restaurant that serves international cuisine, a bar, many shops, tennis, golf, and even a private Club de Playa (*Club La Concha*) with its own restaurant and swimming pool. The beach club, located on the bay and curiously lacking a beach, provides free shuttle service to and from guests' rooms. For guests with a back-to-nature disposition, the hotel has its own rental jeeps, which may be hired at the modest sum of 493 pesos per day, insurance and fuel included, for junkets within a 30-kilometre radius around the bay (Pie de la Cuesta or Barra Vieja). Entry into this little corner of paradise requires a daily admission fee of 1,940 to 2,745 pesos for simple units, or 3,240 to 4,315 for luxury rooms and villa suites.

The 1,019 rooms of the **Acapulco Princess** hotel *($$$$-$$$$$; pb, tv, ≡, ≈, ☺, ℜ; Playa Revolcadero, Apto 1351, C.P. 39300, ☎ 69-10-00 or toll free in the U.S. and Canada 1-800-223-18-18, ≠ 69-10-16)* are distributed in two imposing pyramid-shaped buildings reminiscent of Mayan temples. In an

enclave in the heart of an expansive golf course facing Playa Revolcadero, famous for its powerful waves, the buildings are decorated with flourishing plants that seem to be progressively overgrowing the terraces. In front of the main building (the pyramid-shaped one) is a magnificent flowering garden that appears to have been lovingly designed by a landscape architect. Cascades flowing from pool to pool and a little suspension bridge complete this dream vision of palm trees and bougainvillaea proliferating unrestrained. As though to intensify the exotic quality of the site, flocks of swans and pink flamingos have taken residence here. The rooms are all equipped with elegant furnishings but the modesty of the bathrooms in the standard units, which are nonetheless perfectly adequate, contrasts slightly with the overall decor of the rooms. Those who can treat themselves to the Marquesa Executive Suite ($300 US + IVA in the low season) may contemplate the sea and the backcountry simultaneously from an immense private patio in a setting where luxury is the art of living. Tennis, golf, horseback riding, windsurfing and many other sports are possible here, for a fee of course. Stores, travel agencies, bars, restaurants, a cafeteria, a nightclub, etc.: there is nothing lacking in this isolated compound. Located near the airport, a visitor could spend an entire holiday here without even realizing that on the other side of the bay exists a bustling, vibrant city. The shortest of trips from the complex requires a car or taxi and the only possible escape, without cost, is limited to visits of other buildings such as **Pierre Marqués**, another hotel in the same chain. This holiday formula is most appreciated by travellers in search of relaxation and tranquillity.

Tour B: Pie de la Cuesta

Some rudimentary and poorly sound-proofed rooms, offered with a smiling, friendly welcome await at **Casa Blanca** *($; bd, ⊗; Pie de la Cuesta, ocean side, C.P. 39300, ☎ 60-03-24)*. This location is suitable for those travelling with very restrained budgets. A double room is 120 pesos.

The modest hotel **Playa Leonor** *($; bd, ⊗; Pie de la Cuesta, on the main street heading north, ☎ 60-03-48)* rents simply furnished rooms in a plain decor at particularly good rates (starting at 120 pesos).

Hotel Ukae Kim *($$$; bd, ≈, ℜ; Pie de la Cuesta, on the left side of the main street heading north, ☎ 60-21-87, ⚏ 60-21-88)*. This hotel, which is actually a collection of small two-story cottages nestled in a verdant garden, does not have a direct view of the sea but is located two steps from the beach. Every unit is painted in bright colours and decorated with dot motifs, which adds lots of character. The furniture is simple and the rooms are modestly equipped. Credit cards are not accepted.

Among the all-inclusive packages is the large **Parador del Sol** complex *($$$$; bd, tv, ≡, ≈, ℜ; Pie de la Cuesta, Barra de Coyuca, Apto 1070,   C.P. 39300, ☎ 60-20-03, ⚏ 60-16-49)*, which comprises 75 bungalows spread between the lagoon and the coast and surrounded by lovely gardens. While 43 units are located on the Pacific shore, the 32 others open onto the peaceful Coyuca lagoon. A small footbridge provides passage from one side to the other. The decoration of the rooms is standard and unsurprising, and the furnishings are adequate but not particularly luxurious.

RESTAURANTS

Tour A: Bahía Marqués and Environs

Located behind the La Vista shopping mall, the restaurant-bar **Señor Frog's** *($$; Carretera Escénica, near the La Vista shopping mall, ☎ 84-80-20, 84-80-27)* appears to be the main meeting-place of Acapulco anglophiles. From the menu to the posters to the music, everything here breathes North American pop culture and about the only things that are Mexican are the drinks (margaritas and tequila flow freely) and the few dishes that are served. In the evening, music plays at ear-piercing volume and tourists mingle cheerfully with local young people avid about anything that seems "made in the USA".

Just next door to the very select Spicey, **Kookaburra** *($$$; every day 6pm to midnight; Carretera Escénica, facing the Las Brisas hotel, ☎ 84-14-48 or 84-44-18)* also offers a terrace with a view, but it is less elegant and the view is decidedly not as panoramic as that of its competitor. The cuisine here is typical,

proposing traditional meat and fish dishes that are available in many bay restaurants. The main advantage of this establishment is its prices, which are more reasonable than those of its neighbours. Reservations are recommended.

Miramar *($$$$; Carretera Escénica, near the Las Brisas hotel, on the right side of the road heading toward Puerto Marqués,* ☎ *84-78-74 or 84-78-75)*. After crossing a threshold of questionable tastefulness, wide stairs lead down to a large terrace, covered by an impressive wooden rotunda roof. The view is literally breathtaking and can be enjoyed by almost all of the diners on the semi-circular terrace. The decor, which is a lighthearted combination of sky blue and candy pink can only be described as kitsch. The fare holds few surprises, most of the classics of French cuisine are listed on the menu. The price/quality ratio here is average but the extraordinary view is a definite plus.

Due to its exceptional panoramic view of the bay and its wonderful decor, **Madeiras** *($$$$; Carretera Escénica, near the Las Brisas luxury hotel, on the right side of the road heading toward Puerto Marqués,* ☎ *84-43-78 or 84-73-16)* is very popular, so much so that reservations are recommended, especially to have a table with a view. Cooled by the evening breeze and seated at ample tables, diners savour refined cuisine. Candlelight, omnipresent wood accents and soft music ensure an elegant setting. The menu proposes a formula of four courses that prove irresistible. To start there is the choice of a refreshing green salad or a surprising strawberry soup. Then comes octopus and squid *ensalada* served with *nopales* (see p 48) with an apple vinaigrette, or a succulent *Tamal al Chipotte* (corn dough stuffed with chicken and served with avocado purée all in a mild chipotte sauce). As a main dish, *pechuga al pato* (breast of duck) or *Huachinango Quetzal* (red snapper served on a bed of *nopales* with black bean sauce, accompanied by a few shrimp) are but two of the options. To accompany these delights, try a local wine, such as the excellent *blanc de blanc* (white from white grapes) from Domeck (95 pesos), as imported wines are very expensive in Mexico. As for the service, while it is very professional, the hurry with which tables are cleared is lamentable. The restaurant is owned by the artist Emilia Castillo, daughter of Antonio Castillo, who was the apprentice of the celebrated William Spratling (see p 122). Among the creations which may be

admired here are the stunning wine list, with its silver cover, the dishes and the extravagant wine bucket. Her shop, where many of her other creations are sold, is located at the entrance to the restaurant. Excellent price/quality ratio.

Among restaurants with extraordinary settings, **Spicey** *($$$$$;* *Carretera Escénica, facing the Las Brisas hotel,* ☎ *81-13-80 and* *81-04-70)* earns top prize. Astonishingly, it is neither its furnishings nor any particular decoration that make this a unique site, but rather its setting, a completely open terrace on the roof of a little building that literally overhangs the bay. Visitors have the impression of being actors, surrounded as they are by such dramatic scenery, a thousand sparkling lights illuminating the far-off bay. As for the cuisine, the owners play the exoticism card by offering dishes of fish and meat with flavourings of Thailand, India and even California. Unfortunately a certain pretentiousness emanates from the place (evening wear is required) and is accompanied by unjustly high prices.

Tour B: Pie de la Cuesta

Restaurante Las Tres Marias *($$; on the main street along the lagoon, on the right side heading west).* This restaurant possesses two sections actually divided by the main street. The ocean side is obviously more pleasant for its location facing the sea, but is hindered by the constant disruptions of passing vendors. The dining area across the street is in the heart of a building to which entrance is strictly controlled, and which opens onto Coyuca lagoon, reminiscent of the peaceful lake Chapala (in Jalisco state). Here, diners can enjoy a quiet lunch on a lovely terrace sheltered by a palm-frond roof and decorated with crafts. The seafood cocktail is particularly refreshing and the dishes are enjoyable and served without fuss. This is a perfect spot for a meal away from the crowds of the Costera.

ENTERTAINMENT

Bars and Nightclubs

Tour A: Bahía Marqués and Environs

Leaving the end of the Costera, from the Hyatt hotel, and climbing Carretera Escénica, there are many mega-nightclubs that have the peculiar tendency to charge progressively higher admission fees the further up the hill they are located! Most ask between $15 US and $20 US and more, which sometimes does not even include a drink. These establishments are mainly frequented by tanned young people and strict dress codes apply. Goodbye to shorts, sandals and t-shirts! Here are a few addresses:

The least expensive and least strict in terms of dress is **News** *(admission includes open bar; on the Costera, near the Hyatt)*. With a capacity of 1,200 people it is preferable to go on the weekend (big nights out!) than to see the place half-deserted. There is unoriginal English-language music and the decor is a bit tacky.

Ensconced in a large, cubical building, completely illuminated in pink neon, **Extravaganzza** *(admission; Carretera Escénica, on the left side heading toward the Las Brisas hotel)* is impossible to miss. Despite its respectable size and its capacity of 700 people, this nightclub is practically dwarfed by its neighbouring competitors. The dress code is applied to the letter and except for Wednesdays (open bar for national drinks) the cover charge includes no beverages. On Saturdays free promotional t-shirts are offered to those who present an invitation (sometimes available at hotels), after payment of the admission fee of course! With its slogan that rings false, "Lifestyles of the Rich and Famous", it goes without saying that not every one will feel at ease in this perfect world.

If your goal is to meet passing celebrities, do not miss **Fantasy** *(admission; Carretera Escénica, in the La Vista shopping mall, on the right side heading toward the Las Brisas hotel)*, the

pinnacle of high style and good looks. Set smiles, open wallets, see and be seen!

Finally, **Palladium** *(admission; Carretera Escénica, on the left heading toward the airport)* puts technology to work in the service of entertainment! With a giant window looking over the bay, this nightclub is one of the largest of all. Imagine 1,500 people, in a shower of lasers, swaying their hips to the sounds of the latest hits howling out of huge speakers and you have a good idea of the kind of night that awaits.

TAXCO

Located 205 kilometres north of Acapulco, the city of Taxco is renowned in Mexico as home to the impressive church of Santa Prisca, a veritable masterpiece of baroque art, and to numerous silverware shops, which bear witness to the rich history of the local mining industry. Strolling through narrow alleys lined with lovely little houses, their roofs covered in Mediterranean-style tiles, is a genuine pleasure. As well, sightseers may take advantage of beautiful views of surrounding mountains, including 2,220-metre "El Atachi", which seems to be observing from afar the flurry of tourist activity. Exploration of the city can prove perilous for some, so steep are the cobbled streets. Taxco, in fact, practically clings to the side of mount Atachi, whose native name means "lord of the waters" and is an allusion to the enormous volume of run-off water that rushes down from the mountain during the rainy season.

Visitors make the refreshing excursion to Taxco from tropical Acapulco in order to discover one of the most beautiful colonial cities in Mexico. With an average temperature of 21°C during the day and of 18°C at night, this city enjoys a perfect climate for exploratory outings.

HISTORY

In the 15th century, the powerful ruler Montezuma definitively conquered the region south of Mexico City. The name *Tlachco* appeared then for the first time on the map of his empire. In the native language, *Tlachco* means "place where people play ball", and the name "Taxco" is derived from this word. The Aztec conquest proved to be short-lived, as, beginning in 1524, the Spanish captains Rodrigo de Castañeda and Miguel Díaz de Auz began seizing the region. According to some historians, it was references in native lore of the presence of metals in these lands that precipitated the arrival of the Spanish. At that time, in fact, the conquistadors had a pressing need of metal for the production of cannons necessary to the defense of newly conquered territories. Despite the discovery of precious metals in 1528, it was not until 1534 that the first silver mine appeared, in a locality called "Tetelcingo" (today Taxco el Viejo), 12 kilometres from present-day Taxco. Simultaneously, the Spanish crown created in New Spain the Reales de Minas, a sort of royal mining authority that was charged with the task of ensuring the crown's portion of mine revenues. The mining industry was entrusted to colonists (in general nobles), while the labour force was comprised of native people reduced to slavery. In 1539, a mining regulation dictated the end of the use of native people as slaves and imposed salaried remuneration for them. As this new ruling applied only to natives, owners turned to the importation of African people, and Taxco became one of the largest mines in New Spain to exploit black slaves. In about 1570, Reales de Minas administered three large mines in the region: Tetelcingo, San Miguel and Acayotla, of which only Tetelcingo was developed on a large scale. The situation remained stable until the end of the 16th century when an uprising took place, punctuated by riots followed by severe repression, which resulted in the escape of almost all of the slaves to other regions of Mexico. The black Christ of Santa Prisca cathedral is today the only remaining, visible evidence of an era when Taxco was the setting of an extraordinary mix of populations. Despite this troubled period, Taxco continued to benefit from extraordinary economic development, with major gold-bearing discoveries in a period that extends from the 17th to the 18th century. Among the men who indelibly marked the history of the region, Don José de la Borda is perhaps the most illustrious. Through the acquisition of various mines, he

amassed a considerable personal fortune, which was used to erect one of the most beautiful cathedrals in Mexico, Santa Prisca.

José de la Borda

Don José de la Borda was born in France at Oleran (in the French Pyrenees) January 2nd, 1699. Born of a French father but living in Spain, at the age of 17 years he decided to join his brother Francisco, then freshly emigrated to New Spain in the aim of running a mine. When he arrived in Taxco in 1617, his brother was excavating a deposit in Tehuilotepec, a mine in which Borda decided to invest. The discovery of a large deposit in 1728 marked the beginning of his fortune. He inherited this mine after the death of his brother, and then discovered another deposit at San Ignacio. He capably formed associations with other miners, through which he obtained the discovery of other deposits, these at Pachuca. A skilled technician, Borda introduced not only new mining methods and the first steps toward mechanization, but was also responsible for supplying the city with potable water and constructing various roads to facilitate transport of merchandise. Particularly devout, he perceived his financial success as the work of God and decided to use his personal fortune to erect Santa Prisca cathedral. He imposed his own will in plans for the cathedral, a unique situation at a time when this privilege was reserved for the Catholic Church and the royal family. As well, his son, Manuel de la Borda, was the first priest to recite mass at the cathedral. Work on the cathedral lasted from 1751 to 1759, only eight years, another achievement considering the colossal scale of the undertaking. Nonetheless, costs occasioned by the hiring of approximately one hundred artisans for the construction of the cathedral and of his luxurious home consumed the better part of his assets. At the age of 71 years, a few years before his death, Don José put his faith in Providence again and invested all that was left of his fortune in a new mine in Zacatecas. He died at the age of 79 years, having discovered a new vein and built a new fortune, his convictions confirmed.

Through the 19th century, silver mines gradually lost importance, while the city participated gloriously in the country's war of independence. When at the beginning of the 20th century Taxco seemed to be drifting away from its image of past glory, an American man named William Spratling brought renewal, the outgrowth of which continues to thrive in the city today. After establishing himself here in 1931, this artist founded a great silversmithing school and, in just a few years, succeeded in making a veritable local industry of it. In 1937, the first silver fair, later to become an annual event, marked the beginning of a tradition and opened the road toward global recognition of Taxco as a city of art. Since, numerous creative silversmiths have gravitated to this city, and the shops have not ceased to multiply. Today Taxco offers visitors not only the most beautiful silver art objects in the country, but also a marvellously preserved colonial city, with one of the purest baroque jewels of New Spain at its centre: Santa Prisca cathedral.

 FINDING YOUR WAY AROUND

By Car

Situated in the heart of a mountainous region, Taxco possesses a network of very steep alleys that are covered in paving stones. Throughout the day, countless "Beetle" taxis climb the little streets of the city with astonishing ease, carrying at times as many as six passengers per vehicle! To further complicate things, residents sometimes park their vehicles on the streets, rendering passageways particularly narrow. All this to say that traffic in the centre of Taxco is very difficult to negotiate, and we recommend that travellers avoid coming here by car.

Those who do opt for car travel should avoid driving downtown, in respect for residents, and rather select one of the many *estacionamientos* in which they may park their vehicles. Most attractions are easily accessible on foot, and travellers can gain the satisfaction of having contributed to the quality of life and the environment of Taxco. Be aware that there are no sidewalks downtown, these having been replaced by a simple white line delimiting pedestrian lanes. Also take note that most of the streets of Taxco are one-way.

To reach Taxco from Acapulco or from the north, take toll highway 95D (commonly known as "Autopista del Sol") to the intersection with the new highway that leads directly to Taxco.

By Bus and by Taxi

It would seem, to traffic observers, that only two types of vehicles are driven in Taxco. One is the famous Volkswagen Beetle, with its amusing shape, which is generally used for taxis. The other is also a Volkswagen: the "combi" type which can accommodate up to 10 passengers. In Taxco this last serves the same purpose as do big buses in other cities. The "buses" of Taxco provide service every day, from 7am to 9pm, and stop at most of the *plazas* of the city *(count on 0.50 centavos per trip)*. Taxis are not equipped with metres, and the generally fixed price varies as a function of destination. Since everything is nearby in Taxco, it is rare to pay more than 15 pesos per trip.

By Bus

The Estrella de Oro bus line counts among the most reliable and its buses are equipped with toilets. Some have televisions, and some even provide free coffee dispensers. Among the destinations serviced by this operator are Chilpancingo (the capital of the State of Guerrero), Acapulco, Cuernavaca, México (the federal capital) and Ixtapa-Zihuatanejo.

Unfortunately, the firm does not sell return tickets, and each ticket must therefore be purchased at the departure station. Moreover, unlike the sales offices of Acapulco, those in Taxco do not accept credit cards. Seats are assigned during the high season and weekends, so it is preferable to reserve ahead of time, especially for travellers who prefer particular seats and who want to avoid being jostled about. Once arrived at the destination, travellers should plan for their return tickets. Budget for between 80 and 100 pesos one-way to Acapulco, depending on the class of bus.

In Taxco:
Terminal Estrella de Oro
Av. J.F. Kennedy, sometimes also called "Avenida de los Plateros"
At the entrance to the village, down below.

In Acapulco:
Terminal Estrella de Oro
Av. Cuauhtémoc 158 *(corner of Avenida Wilfrido Massieu)*
Take any bus marked Base-Cine Río-Caleta
(on foot or by car, take the Costera to reach the Gran Plaza Acapulco shopping centre, head east on Avenida Wilfrido Massieu and pass a large block of houses)
☎ 85-87-05

PRACTICAL INFORMATION

Tourist Information

While there are two tourist offices in Taxco, only one of them is really equipped to provide information on the spot:

Secretaría de Turismo
Av. J.F. Kennedy (just next to the arch overhanging the main street)
☎ 2-66-16

Mail and Telecommunications

Correo Mexpost
Av. J.F. Kennedy
Just east of Terminal de Estrella de Oro

Useful Telephone Numbers

The area code for Taxco is **762**.

Police: ☎ 2-22-74 or 2-00-07

Hospital

Clínica San José
☎ 2-55-75

Pharmacies

There are at least ten pharmacies in Taxco – it is not difficult to find one on each of the main streets in town.

Money and Banking

Bancomer
Calle Cuauhtémoc, on the left heading toward Plazuela San Juan.
VISA card withdrawals are possible at the automatic teller.

Spanish Courses

UNAM (Universidad Nacional Autónoma de México)
Ex-Hacienda El Chorrillo
Apartado 70
40200 Taxco, Guerrero
Mexico
☎ and ≈ 2-01-24

 EXPLORING

The best way to visit Taxco is to stroll along its charming cobbled streets, making use now and then of the many, occasionally very steep, stairways. As a guide for discovery of the town, a tour that can easily be accomplished in one day is described below.

The tour of Taxco begins at the entrance to the village, near Barrio Cena Obscura, where the Estrella de Oro bus station is

located *(Av J.F. Kennedy, previously called "Avenida de los Plateros")*.

During the colonial era, Avenida J.F. Kennedy, or **"Avenida de los Plateros"**, was an important thoroughfare for the transport of precious silver ore from various mines. At that time a checkpoint was established at the corner of Plaza de la Garita where every commercial vehicle entering the town was inspected and the royal share of the merchandise was collected.

Walk toward Calle de la Pilita, situated across from the bus station, and follow it to Calle Carlos J. Nibbi, which leads directly to Plazuela San Juan.

With a lovely fountain at its centre and a cobbled court on which is outlined a large white star, **Plazuela San Juan ★★ (1)** could be described as a sort of "mini Place de l'Étoile", like the one in Paris, so heavy is the traffic. An entertaining procession of little "Beetles" and vans may be observed here, loading and unloading housekeepers, merchants, civil servants and business people at a constant rhythm. At this square, Taxco has the look of a metropolis full of activity, which is not unremarkable given the relatively modest size of the town. The effect is even more amusing seen from above on one of the little balconies of the restaurant El Adobe (see p 140), which also provide a wonderful view of the steeples of Santa Prisca in the distance.

Still on the square, stroll to the north side to admire **Casa Grande ★ (2)** *(Plazuela San Juan)*, an important 18th-century colonial house. Although it has been renovated several times over, it preserves a magnificent interior patio, embellished by imposing columns. Do not hesitate to go upstairs, where the scale of it can be better appreciated. Various shops, a restaurant and a hotel are maintained in the house.

Before taking Calle Cuauhtémoc, climb little Callejón del Nogal, located immediately to the right of Casa Grande, for a brief visit of **Casa del Nogal** (on the left-hand side of the street), which according to legend was built by the regrettably well-known pirate Francis Drake.

Take Calle Cuauhtémoc in the direction of Plaza Borda, the "Zócalo".

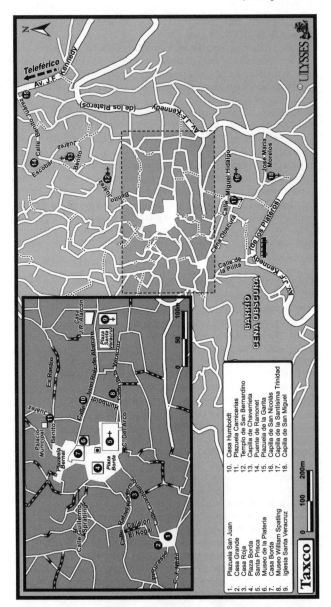

Taxco

1. Plazuela San Juan
2. Casa Grande
3. Casa Roja
4. Plaza Borda
5. Santa Prisca
6. Museo de la Platería
7. Casa Borda
8. Museo William Spratling
9. Iglesia Santa Veracruz
10. Casa Humboldt
11. Plazuela Carnicerías
12. Templo de San Bernardino
13. Capilla de Chavarrieta
14. Puente de Ramonet
15. Plazuela de la Garita
16. Capilla de San Nicolás
17. Capilla de la Santísima Trinidad
18. Capilla de San Miguel

Mid-way along very commercial Calle Cuauhtémoc, on the left, is **Casa Roja (3)** *(Calle Cuauhtémoc)*, which was once painted red and which is also known as "Casa Verdugo", after the maiden name of the wife of vcelebrated Don José de la Borda's wife's maiden name. In addition to certain members of the couple's family, many of Taxco's inquisitors have lived here.

Succeeding its "little sister" just nearby (Plazuela San Juan), **Plaza Borda ★★★ (4)**, familiarly called "El Zócalo", constitutes the very heart of the town. Its centre beautified by a small garden, it is furnished with benches that make excellent perches from which to people watch. Town residents often make dates to meet here, and vendors of all sorts roam the square looking for tourists. Crowds of visitors from the capital frequent Taxco and on weekends it is not unusual for young people to assemble here, radio cassette players in hand, and dance to the sounds of disco music. A fountain dating from 1741 as well as a bust of José de la Borda complete the design of the Zócalo.

The sight that provides true majesty to this square, rising from its west side, is the sumptuous façade of **Santa Prisca ★★★ (5)**. A genuine masterpiece of baroque art, the cathedral was erected between 1750 and 1758 on the initiative of a rich silver-mine owner, Don José de la Borda (see p 121). According to some, the architect Cayetano de Sigüenza drew up the plans for the church, which was constructed on the site of a small church once dedicated to Saint Sebastian. The cathedral benefits from two protectors: San Sebastián and Santa Prisca, two martyrs of the Roman nobility. Its two patrons are represented on either side of the central medallion, framed by exquisite wreathed columns.

Upon close observation of the cathedral's pinkish-tinted stone façade, it is impossible to miss the astonishing contrast between the rich decoration of the central part of the building and the almost total absence of ornamentation at the base of the two lateral towers. This disparity is made even stranger by the fact that the tops of these last are laden with designs. With this ingenious device the designer of the building lightened the massive aspect of the church and created the illusion of greater height. In all their splendour, the two Andalusian-style steeples stand gracefully in the sky framing an elegant Puebla ceramic-tile dome. The presence in the façade itself of numerous

Catedral Santa Prisca

The Baroque in Service of Colonization

According to some historians, the tremendous spread of baroque art in New Spain originated not in any particular admiration on the part of colonizers for this art form, but rather was an outgrowth of their desire to perfect the Conquest. A particularly narrative style, baroque art was a formidable instrument of integration. At first purely territorial, the project of colonization came up against the reality of the diversity of peoples and beliefs in the region. Combining images of saints, angels and cherubim with more pagan elements such as representations of flora and fauna (some of which are purely local), no style was a more suitable medium of propaganda. Belief in local deities such as Atachi (the god of the waters) was effectively supplanted by a saintly Prisca, patroness of the storms, protectress from lightening and floods. As well, the practice of making offerings found its equivalent in the many thanksgivings that were hung in churches. Finally, certain façade bas-reliefs are explicitly designed to convey messages, like simple "advertisements". An example of this, the imposing central medallion laid out on the façade of Santa Prisca represents the baptism of Christ, clearly implying that to enter the church, and thereby the kingdom of heaven and abundance (this last being suggested by the richness of the exterior decoration), one must first be baptized. Baroque art was here an instrument of assimilation, and thereby of achieving the ends of colonization.

cherubim as well as motifs such as shells and volutes is a characteristic of baroque art in New Spain.

Another unique characteristic is that underneath extremely lavish decoration is hidden a structure of exceptionally pure style, erected in a single stroke, so to speak. While this element might seem inconsequential, it is worth mentioning since in this era building projects of this magnitude were subject to the influence of the various styles favoured by each generation of Church officials under whose authority they fell. It is thus normal to see many styles superimposed upon one another in edifices of this scale, yet this is not the case here. The style of

this cathedral is that of an entrepreneurial man, rigorous in its use of form and space.

The harmonious interior of the cathedral encloses 12 churrigueresque **retables** ★★★, made entirely of painted wood and gold leaf, and laid out as follows: on either side of the central nave six retables are placed facing each other. Each of them represents one or more biblical figures in order of increasing biblical importance approaching the high altar. Further, on either side of the transept this time, two more retables representing the **Virgen de la Guadelupe** (on the left) and the **Virgen del Rosario** (on the right) merit attention. Their placement in proximity to the high altar is not insignificant but rather reflects the importance accorded these two figures by ecclesiastic powers. The fact that the Virgin of Guadalupe (patron saint of Mexico) and the Virgin of the Rosary (adulated by the Spanish church) have been placed facing each other symbolizes the desire of the church to unify the two worlds. The masterpiece, the **high altar** ★★★, imposes the divine order: Saint Peter, the various popes, followed by the apostles, evangelists, and lastly the Doctors of the Church. In the left side chapel, three final retables complete the impressive catalog created by the Brothers Isodoro Vicente and Luis de Balbás, and the artisans Don Juan Joseph de Alva and Juan Caballero.

The **sacristy** and the **chapter house** ★ for their part are home to a series of paintings representing religious scenes and notable Taxco natives, including José de la Borda and his son Manuel. A little shop with religious souvenirs is located in proximity to the chapter house.

Head toward the small Calle de los Muertos, situated directly to the left of the church.

A brief stroll on **Calle de los Muertos** permits a glimpse of a curious little statue of an armless human skeleton, which overhangs the entrance to the bell tower and the ossuary. At one time the bodies of the dead were transported along this street and through this door, hence its name, "the street of the dead".

Located at the northeast end of Plaza Borda, **Museo de la Plateria (6)** *(3 pesos; Tue to Sun 10am to 5pm; to reach the museum entrance, cross to the end of the shopping arcade and*

take the small stairway that leads to the basement) houses a small exhibition room in which is displayed a collection of antique silver pieces created by local artisans. As this book went to press, however, the museum was closed for restoration work. As well be aware that on the way to the staircase that leads to the museum entrance many shopkeepers attempt to lure in tourists by claiming that the museum is located in their stores!

Just next door to Museo de la Plateria, **Casa Borda (7)** *(entrance on the north side of the Zócalo)* dates from 1759 and is actually two houses. While the façade on the Zócalo permits access to the former residence of Don José de la Borda, behind and below that building, on Plaza Bernal, is the house that belonged to his son, Manuel de la Borda. Today various administrative offices as well as a cultural centre are located here. The interior is worth a visit above all for its **lovely patio** ★, the centre of which is adorned with an exquisite baroque fountain.

Retrace your steps, and take Callejón del Arco, situated immediately to the right of Santa Prisca cathedral.

After descending picturesque Callejón del Arco and passing under the archway connecting the presbytery to Santa Prisca, the route reaches the small Plazuela Hidalgo, the site of **Museo William Spratling ★★★ (8)** *(10 pesos; Tue to Sun 10am to 5pm; corner of Calle de la Veracruz and Calle Humboldt, behind Santa Prisca cathedral)*. Founded in 1975, this museum houses a collection of sculptures, jewellery and other pre-Columbian objects acquired by the American artist William Spratling (see also p 122). While the exhibition emphasizes the aesthetic and informative aspects rather than the historical, not all of the pieces exhibited being authentic, a visit is no less rewarding given the quality of the reproductions. The many descriptive texts are in Spanish only; a meagre English information pamphlet is available at the entrance. Among the more noteworthy pieces is a preclassical, *guerrero* stele, at the entrance, representing very geometric figures and, just beside it, an odd sculpture of a woman squatting in childbirth. Some very interesting jewellery pieces made of *concha de caracol* (conch shell) are also exhibited.

Exiting the museum, it is impossible to miss the busts of Hidalgo (hero of Mexican independence), on the Plazuela proper, and of the famous playwright Juan Ruiz de Alarcón, whose name is sometimes linked to that of the town (Taxco de Alarcón).

Continue to descend Calle de la Veracruz to the next church and skirt around it on the east side to reach Plaza de la Santa Veracruz.

With its bare façade and its uninteresting interior, **Iglesia Santa Veracruz (9)** merits the detour mainly for its **lovely square ★**, entirely decorated with little coloured stones. Facing it, **Casa de Juan Ruiz de Alarcón** was, according to legend, where the renown writer was born in 1580.

Go back up Calle Juan Ruiz de Alarcón to the crossroads with Calle Porfirio A. Delgado, also called "Calle Humboldt".

Of all the colonial homes in Taxco, **Casa Humboldt ★★★ (10)** has probably preserved the greatest charm. Its **façade ★★★**, composed of elegant *mudéjar*-inspired motifs, makes the trip worthwhile in itself. The house is named for Baron Alexander von Humboldt (1769-1859), a German naturalist who, through the observations he made during his travels, contributed greatly to a better knowledge of the climate, the oceans and geology. He resided here during his first journey between Mexico City and Acapulco. Restored in 1991, the building now houses the **Museo de Arte Sacro Virreinal ★★** *(10 pesos; Tue to Sun 10am to 5pm; Calle Juan Ruiz de Alarcón)*, which is dedicated to religious art. Even travellers who are not passionate about this type of art should not miss visiting this house as it is a wonderful example of a colonial residence, and the excellent restoration work is also worth seeing. Above all do not miss the *tímulos funerarios* on the ground floor, a curious, wooden funerary stele on several levels, each of which is decorated with paintings, sculptures or floral ornamentation. Due to their great cost, such stelae were above all erected for members of the nobility or important personages. In some cases, the coffin of the deceased was placed inside, at the centre of the stele. The one exhibited here was miraculously discovered under Santa Prisca during the restoration of the building in 1988. One exhibition room is dedicated to Baron von Humboldt, and most of the information panels are written in Spanish and in English.

Casa Humboldt

Continue the ascent of Calle Juan Ruiz de Alarcón to Plazuela Bernal, where you can admire the back of Casa Borda, a particularly impressive sight from here. Then take Calle Benito Juárez, northeast of the square.

Once called "Calle Real", **Calle Benito Juárez** ★★ is one of the most picturesque and winding streets in Taxco; meandering along it is a true pleasure. Many admirable homes on this street, while not of great historical importance, have maintained all the charm of the colonial era. A number of *plazas* succeed each other along this street, on which strollers may stop to better take in the sights of the area. Sidewalks here meld with the cobbles of the street and are creatively demarcated with white paving-stones, as are traffic directions, on the ground itself.

The first square on this street is **Plazuela Carnicerias (11)**. In addition to interesting designs on the ground representing the **game of pelota ★**, the old city hall of Taxco, decorated with a **mural**, may also be admired here.

Two steps away, past a little bend, **Plaza del Exconvento** opens on **Templo de San Bernardino (12)**. Despite its location on a lovely square, this church, which has been renovated many times and has a rather damaged façade, offers little of interest other than a few religious paintings and sculptures.

Further along, Calle Benito Juárez skirts around a hillock at the summit of which stands **Capilla de Chaverrieta ★ (13)**. This lovely chapel is accessible via stairs built right to the main street. In addition to the captivating view from the square, this chapel presents beautiful pink-tinted stone quatrefoiled **columns**. Also worth mentioning is its finely worked, sculpted wood **entrance door**.

Return to Calle Benito Juárez, which ends its course in a straight line, crossing **Puente de Ramonet (14)** (1880) to **Plazuela de la Garita (15)**, once a checkpoint for merchandise entering and leaving the city.

Other Attractions

Capilla San Nícolas (14), which dates from the beginning of the 18th century, but has undergone much work over the course of the centuries, features an appealing **wood balcony** overhanging its main entrance.

Facing this last chapel, past a little park, **Capilla de la Santísima Trinidad (15)** is, according to some, the oldest religious building in Taxco. Erected near the end of the 16th century, its exterior completely preserves its original appearance, contrary to its interior which has unfortunately been renovated many times over. As this book went to press, the building was not accessible due to restoration work.

Still in proximity to Capilla San Nícolas, at the minibus stations, there is a little gallery that leads to a beautiful **lookout ★★** over Santa Prisca and nearby houses.

Standing on the lovely plazuela of the same name, **Capilla de San Miguel (16)** features a harmonious façade and **baroque steeple ★**. Unfortunately, yet again the interior of this chapel holds no particular appeal due to numerous modifications.

For lovers of panoramic views and those who have a little extra time, an ascent to the summit of La Cantera (1,930 m) by means of the **Teleférico (17)** *(15 pesos one-way, 22 pesos return; every day 8am to 7pm; Av. J. F. Kennedy, facing the tourist office, just past Los Arcos)* is an agreeable excursion. The cool peak of this mountain provides magnificent **views ★★** over Taxco, as well as a pleasant terrace where visitors may quench their thirst. More adventurous types can climb La Cantera via a paved road near Avenida J.F. Kennedy or "Avenida de los Plateros". Count on between 30 minutes and one hour to reach the summit.

 ACCOMMODATIONS

Despite its setting in a beautiful colonial building complete with a patio with sculpted columns, **Hotel Casa Grande** *($; Plazuela San Juan no. 7, Altos, upstairs from Casa Grande, ☎ and ⇆ 2-11-8)* offers rudimentary, dark, and poorly soundproofed rooms. The rooms that seem most acceptable are those on the very top floor, the roof. As well as being bright, these rooms allow guests to take advantage at any hour of the rooftop terrace and the magnificent view it offers. Ask to see the room before renting it.

As its name indicates, **Hotel Los Arcos** *($; pb; Calle Juan Ruíz de Alarcón no. 2, ☎ 2-18-36, ⇆ 2-32-11)* possesses an interior patio embellished by lovely archways, prettily adorned with flowers and decorated with stylish furniture. The rooms are clean and pleasant, but some of them (those on the ground floor near the entrance) are dark and uncomfortable due to noise. Ask for one of the rooms on the upper floors, which are brighter and offer a view.

Hotel Posada San Javier *($; ps, ≈; Estacas no. 1, Ex-rastro no. 4, ☎ 2-31-77 or 2-02-31, ⇆ 2-23-51)*. Despite modest furnishings, this hotel is charmingly laid out around a lovely garden in a particularly peaceful environment. The 18 rooms are distributed in cabins, most with little terraces. While some rooms

have enchanting views and are particularly well-insulated, others are located near the reception desk and do not offer much intimacy. It is thus strongly recommended to ask to see the room before making a decision. The hotel is off in a little alley and does not announce itself with many signs, so it is a little difficult to find. To reach it, take Calle Benito Juárez, and go down the steep stairway just facing Palacio Municipal. The entrance to the hotel is on the left side of the street, across from Farmacia Nueva.

Hotel Santa Prisca *($, suite $$; pb, ℜ; Cena Obscuras no. 1, Apdo 42, on the south side of Plazuela San Juan, ☎ 2-00-80 or 2-09-80, ⬧ 2-29-38).* After walking the long ramp leading from bustling Plazuela San Juan, what a surprise to find oneself suddenly in the middle of a pleasant, flower-filled patio. The rooms of this charming hotel are laid out around a lovely, interior courtyard, adorned with a small fountain and arbours. The rather modest furniture is tasteful and represents a good example of the regional style. Some rooms offer a view of the surrounding valleys. The rooms just next to the ramp accessing the building are to be avoided, though, as they are noisy and do not offer an appealing view.

Maintained in the heart of a series of adjoining buildings, the hotel **Agua Escondida** *($$; ps, ≈; Plaza Borda no.4, corner Calle Guillermo Spratling no. 4, on the north side of the Zócalo, C.P. 40200, ☎ 2-07-26, 2-07-36 or 2-11-66, ⬧ 2-13-06)* rents small, clean, comfortable rooms equipped with lovely, regional-style furniture. While the rooms do not have a direct view of Santa Prisca (some offer a view of nearby streets), the hotel has a succession of terraces, accessible to all, with different views of the surrounding mountains. The only drawback here is the noise of the incessant activity of the Zócalo and of the traffic. Ask to see one of the quieter rooms located around the main patio of the building. Excellent service.

Located not far from Plazuela San Juan, on a hillside, **Hotel Rancho Taxco Victoria** *($$; ps; Calle Carlos J. Nibbi no. 5, 7 y 14, ☎ 2-00-04, 2-10-14 or 2-01-93, ⬧ 2-00-10)* offers the best price/quality ratio in Taxco. As well as providing a beautiful view of Santa Prisca, the rooms benefit from a pleasant terrace with a panorama of the village. Among the rooms with better locations, number 6 is particularly pleasant. The general decor of the hotel is stylish and tasteful. Near the old city but

removed from the noise, the hotel proves ideal for those seeking calm but not isolation.

The largest and most luxurious hotel in Taxco, **Hotel Monte Taxco** *($$$; pb, ≈, tv, ℜ; Fraccionamiento Lomas de Taxco, access via the main street leading to Acapulco, in Taxco ☎ 2-13-00, from Mexico City ☎ 549-77-51 or 549-15-60, ≈ 540-77-02 or 689-15-58, toll-free in Mexico ☎ 91-800-98-00, ≈ 2-14-28)* is perched on a mountain facing the town. Most of its 170 rooms open onto a terrace with a breathtaking view of Taxco and the surrounding valleys. Despite a luxurious entrance, a pool with a view and a pleasant restaurant, the decoration of the rooms lacks character, and the furnishings are quite ordinary. Many activities are proposed here: tennis, horseback riding (30 pesos/hour), gym (20 pesos/hour), aerobics, etc. A cable car close to the hotel provides access to Taxco's main street (Av. J.F. Kennedy). This spot is especially suited to travellers who appreciate seclusion. In the evening, a car or taxi is necessary to reach the centre of Taxco, making a visit to town rather inconvenient. A little expensive for what it offers.

RESTAURANTS

Restaurante de Cruz *($; Calle del Arco, to the left of Santa Prisca church, on the left side of the street going down, just before the arch over the alley)*. This small, unpretentious restaurant possesses a few very ordinary tables where clients can taste *comida corrida* for as little as 20 pesos. A bargain for travellers with limited budgets!

Restaurante Casa Borda *($; at the corner of Casa Borda itself, just before Plazuela Bernal)*. Another little, unassuming restaurant that has a pleasing decor, its particular specialty is iguana. Take note iguana lovers!

Located in the brand new Centro Commercial Plaza Taxco (opened in 1996), **The Italian Coffee Company** *($; every day 8am to 10:30pm; Calle Juan Ruiz de Alarcón, near Casa Humboldt)* offers light cuisine (sandwiches, pastries, croissants, etc.) in a particularly pleasant setting. Seated at a table on the panoramic terrace that offers a view of Templo de San Bernardino and of mount El Atachi (2,220 m) off in the

distance, patrons may also sample one of the restaurant's excellent coffees. A beautiful craft shop (see p 143) lies at the entrance. Not to be missed!

On the ground floor of Centro Commercial Plaza Taxco, the restaurant **Plaza Taxco** *($; every day 8am to 10:30pm; Calle Juan Ruiz de Alarcón, near Casa Humboldt)* prepares simple Mexican dishes for a song (count on 40 pesos for a meal), served on its lovely terrace, in a peaceful setting away from the crowds of the Zócalo.

Whether it is for a *pozole* or for an inexpensive dish of *comida corrida* (20 pesos), **Restaurante San Nicolas** *($; every day 9am to 7pm; Calle Miguel Hidalgo 8a, on the left side of the street heading toward Plazuela San Juan)*, set in a little room of green, white and red colours that brighten an attractive decor, is just the place.

In a warm, traditional ambience, it is a true pleasure to savour the *comida corrida* offered by the very friendly and efficient proprietress of **Restaurante Santa Fe** *($; every day 8am to 11pm; Calle Miguel Hidalgo, on the right side of the street heading toward Plazuela San Juan)*. The *sopa de haba* and broccoli soup are both delicious, and the *torta de camarón con nopalitos* (shrimp and cactus balls) is also noteworthy. Excellent *guacamole*. Budget for 60 pesos for a full meal, and a little less for the *comida corrida*.

The pizza restaurant-bar **Concha Nostra** *($; every day 9am to midnight; on Plazuela San Juan, upstairs from Casa Grande, opposite the entrance of the hotel Casa Grande)* serves delicious pizzas in three sizes (15, 30 or 40 pesos), in a beautiful stone building with stately galleries. The dining room, despite its high ceilings, is intimate and possesses a balcony opening onto the square. A popular meeting place for young people.

The restaurant of the hotel **Santa Prisca** *($; every day 7:30am to 10pm; Cena Obscuras no. 1, Apdo 42, on the south side of Plazuela San Juan)* is eye-catching thanks to its country-style furniture trimmed with small bright blue tablecloths that contrast pleasantly with the brilliant yellow of the rattan chairs. The *cervezas* at six pesos are a bargain!

How to resist the tantalizing and innumerable ice cream flavours scooped up by **Paleteria la Michoacana** *(Calle Cuauhtémoc, on the right side of the street heading toward Plazuela San Juan)*? Pistachio, coconut, mango, papaya, *piña colada*, passion fruit, tamarind and many other flavours are served in cones or as ices.

For early birds, the elegant little terrace decorated with lovely wood and cloth parasols of **Pan Nuestro** *($; Plazuela Bernal)* is a wonderful place to begin the day. The only drawbacks are incessant car traffic and slow service.

The restaurant **Pizza-Pazza** *($; every day 9am to midnight; on the Zócalo, to the right of Santa Prisca)* offers a beautiful side view of Santa Prisca, and, from the balconies, diners can savour tasty pizzas or various Mexican dishes all the while admiring the "belle of the Zócalo". Pizzas between 25 and 45 pesos.

Restaurante Bar Paco *($$; every day 11am to 11pm; on the Zócalo, facing Santa Prisca church)* is the only restaurant on the Zócalo with the privilege of a full view of Santa Prisca. Diners may savour Mexican, Italian, or even Arab cuisine in a beautiful, antique decor embellished by pleasant pastel colours, all under high ceilings and facing very large windows. One of the best times to visit is at about 5pm. Have an aperitif and enjoy the sight of the sun's setting rays reflected on the façade of Santa Prisca, illuminating it with warm colours from pink to soft yellow. Of course, do not expect to have the restaurant all to yourself at this time of day!

Also on the bustling Zócalo, the restaurant **La Parroquia** *($$; every day 10am to 11pm; Plaza Borda, on the west side, entrance by the side street)* offers another view of Santa Prisca, but a rather standard menu of Mexican dishes and an uninteresting decor. This establishment does not accept credit cards.

Restaurante El Adobe *($$$; every day 8am to 11pm; Plazuela San Juan no. 13, corner of Calle Progresso and Carlos J. Nibbi, ☎ 2-14-16)* is an enjoyable restaurant on the third floor of a modest building equipped with elegant, sculpted wood furniture in a decor composed essentially of stone walls, wood ceilings and many green plants. Unfortunately, the presence of a

television somewhat spoils the atmosphere. From tables on either of the two narrow balconies, diners may take advantage of a view of the magnificent steeples of Santa Prisca in the distance and also of Taxco's busy roundabout. Among the dishes proposed, the *queso adobe* (cheese melted over potatoes, onions, sesame and coriander) and the *guerrero* chicken, with peppers, *guacamole*, *frijoles*, onions and sauteed appels, are true delights. For a beautiful ending try the *crepa de cajeta*, a crepe served with caramel sauce. An excellent spot!

The restaurant **El Taxqueño** *($$$$; every day 7am to 11pm; Fraccionamiento Lomas de Taxco, access via the main street leading to Acapulco or via cable car)* is located in the hotel Monte Taxco, on a mountain-top facing Taxco. Here, diners may savour Mexican cuisine and grill dishes in an exquisite atmosphere. The breathtaking view from the hotel, as well as the captivating, spectacular climb by cable car to it, make this an entertaining little gastronomic excursion.

 ENTERTAINMENT

Bars and Nightclubs

Whether it is to begin the evening with an aperitif or to end it with a *digestif*, **El Rincón del Abuelo** *(Calle Cuauhtémoc, on the right side of the street heading toward Plazuela San Juan)* is an ideal spot. Aside from the entrance, framed by two mini-fountains, the decor is modern and elegant featuring black metal furniture and interesting lighting. Unfortunately, as is all too common in bars, a television spoils the charm of the place slightly. Very popular with local young people.

Planet Taxco *(Calle Cuauhtémoc, on the right side of the street heading toward Plazuela San Juan)*. This modern nightclub located in a basement offers *música en vivo*, the style of which varies every week and even sometimes every day (rock, disco, Mexican music, jazz, etc.). Very popular with local young people.

SHOPPING

Thanks to nearby silver mines and the town's silverware manufacturers, Taxco has long been home to many shops. People travel from all over Mexico to buy jewellery, dishes and ornaments made from the precious metal that is the basis of the city's wealth. Boutiques are so numerous that shoppers will have no trouble finding whatever their hearts desire. Here are a few recommendations to keep in mind before setting off on this adventure:

● Know that many of the shops along Av. J.F. Kennedy (the main street leading to Acapulco) are branches of stores located at the centre of Taxco. Unless you are in a hurry, take the time to go the centre of the city, where the ambiance is more pleasant.

● While the city maintains strict control over the quality of silver products sold (it is the root of the area's reputation after all!), check that the stamp MEX 925 (92.5 % silver guaranteed) is well engraved on every object purchased. It can occur that there is not enough space on smaller objects for the stamp. In this case, the seller should remit a certificate guaranteeing the quality of the product. Be aware that the quality of goods bought from peddlers in the street may not be as high.

● Although as a general principle, out of respect for the work of artisans, we recommended against negotiating over prices, silverware merchants of Taxco are for the most part accustomed to this practice. For larger purchases, take your time, compare, and do not hesitate to bargain over the price, you can usually save about 25%. Payment in cash as opposed to credit cards can facilitate the negotiation process.

Here are a few shops with excellent selections of goods and particularly interesting decor:

Lovers of porcelain and silverware should not miss the opportunity to admire the creations of **Emilia Castillo** *(Juan Ruiz de Alarcón 7)*. On the ground floor of the hotel Posada de Los Castillos, shoppers can observe her very original crockery, sculptures and various silver pieces. A descendant of Antonio Castillo, one of the apprentices of famous William Spratling

(see p 122), she has developed a technique by which she inlays silver motifs in porcelain. The result is surprising and absolutely magnificent. A must-see!

Espinosa *(Calle Miguel Hidalgo 7, on the right side of the street heading toward Plazuela San Juan).* It is above all the great variety of objects sold here that attracts attention. Most of the jewellery exhibited here is tasteful, and the staff is particularly friendly.

The shop **David Saúl** *(Calle Cuauhtémoc, on the left side of the street heading toward Plazuela San Juan)* is worth the trip not only for its tremendous selection of jewellery but also for its fanciful decor reproducing the interior of a spotlessly white cave.

For a change from silverware:

Located in the brand new Centro Commercial Plaza Taxco (opened in 1996), **Fonart** *(every day 8am to 10:30pm; Calle Juan Ruiz de Alarcón, near Casa Humboldt)* displays very beautiful craft objects. Knick-knacks, fabric, masks, glassware and many other items have been assembled here by the **Fondo Nacional para el fomento de las Artesianas**, an organization devoted to the promotion of Mexican craftsmanship. The especially pleasant setting is worth visiting and is also an excellent spot to stop for coffee. Not to be missed!

On the patio of Casa Grande, **Artesiana Davila** *(Plazuela San Juan, on the north side of the square)* sells a multitude of lovely painted wooden masks, some of which adorn the entrance to the building.

Near Chaverrieta church and the Farmacia, **Galería San Angel en Taxco** *(Calle Escoba, corner Calle Benito Juárez)* offers an interesting collection of original, modestly priced works. Scented, stylized candles, as well as original ceramics, modern crucifixes, paintings and many other decorative objects may be found here.

GLOSSARY

GREETINGS

Goodbye	*adiós, hasta luego*
Good afternoon and good evening	*buenas tardes*
Hi (casual)	*hola*
Good morning	*buenos días*
Good night	*buenas noches*
Thank you	*gracias*
Please	*por favor*
You are welcome	*de nada*
Excuse me	*perdone/a*
My name is...	*mi nombre es...*
What is your name?	*¿cómo se llama usted?*
yes	*no*
no	*sí*
Do you speak English?	*¿habla usted inglés?*
Slower, please	*más despacio, por favor*
I am sorry, I don't speak Spanish	*Lo siento, no hablo español*
How are you?	*¿qué tal?*
I am fine	*estoy bien*
I am American (male/female)	*Soy estadounidense*
I am Australian	*Soy autraliano/a*
I am Belgian	*Soy belga*
I am British (male/female)	*Soy británico/a*
I am Canadian	*Soy canadiense*
I am German (male/female)	*Soy alemán/a*
I am Italian (male/female)	*Soy italiano/a*
I am Swiss	*Soy suizo*
I am a tourist	*Soy turista*
single (m/f)	*soltero/a*
divorced (m/f)	*divorciado/a*
married (m/f)	*casado/a*
friend (m/f)	*amigo/a*
child (m/f)	*niño/a*
husband, wife	*esposo/a*
mother	*madre*
father	*padre*
brother, sister	*hermano/a*
widower widow	*viudo/a*

I am hungry	*tengo hambre*
I am ill	*estoy enfermo/a*
I am thirsty	*tengo sed*

DIRECTIONS

beside	*al lado de*
to the right	*a la derecha*
to the left	*a la izquierda*
here	*aquí*
there	*allí*
into, inside	*dentro*
outside	*fuera*
behind	*detrás*
in front of	*delante*
between	*entre*
far from	*lejos de*
Where is ... ?	*¿dónde está ... ?*
To get to ...?	*¿para ir a...?*
near	*cerca de*
straight ahead	*todo recto*

MONEY

money	*dinero / plata*
credit card	*tarjeta de crédito*
exchange	*cambio*
traveller's cheque	*cheque de viaje*
I don't have any money	*no tengo dinero*
The bill, please	*la cuenta, por favor*
receipt	*recibo*

SHOPPING

store	*tienda*
market	*mercado*
open	*abierto/a*
closed	*cerrado/a*
How much is this?	*¿cuánto es?*
to buy	*comprar*
to sell	*vender*
the customer	*el / la cliente*
salesman	*vendedor*
saleswoman	*vendedora*
I need...	*necesito...*
I would like...	*yo quisiera...*

batteries	*pilas*
blouse	*blusa*
cameras	*cámaras*
cosmetics and perfumes	*cosméticos y perfumes*
cotton	*algodón*
dress jacket	*saco*
eyeglasses	*lentes, gafas*
fabric	*tela*
film	*película*
gifts	*regalos*
gold	*oro*
handbag	*bolsa*
hat	*sombrero*
jewellery	*joyería*
leather	*cuero, piel*
local crafts	*artesanía*
magazines	*revistas*
newpapers	*periódicos*
pants	*pantalones*
records, cassettes	*discos, casetas*
sandals	*sandalias*
shirt	*camisa*
shoes	*zapatos*
silver	*plata*
skirt	*falda*
sun screen products	*productos solares*
T-shirt	*camiseta*
watch	*reloj*
wool	*lana*

MISCELLANEOUS

a little	*poco*
a lot	*mucho*
good (m/f)	*bueno/a*
bad (m/f)	*malo/a*
beautiful (m/f)	*hermoso/a*
pretty (m/f)	*bonito/a*
ugly	*feo*
big	*grande*
tall (m/f)	*alto/a*
small (m/f)	*pequeño/a*
short (length) (m/f)	*corto/a*
short (person) (m/f)	*bajo/a*
cold (m/f)	*frío/a*

hot	*caliente*
dark (m/f)	*oscuro/a*
light (colour)	*claro*
do not touch	*no tocar*
expensive (m/f)	*caro/a*
cheap (m/f)	*barato/a*
fat (m/f)	*gordo/a*
slim, skinny (m/f)	*delgado/a*
heavy (m/f)	*pesado/a*
light (weight) (m/f)	*ligero/a*
less	*menos*
more	*más*
narrow (m/f)	*estrecho/a*
wide (m/f)	*ancho/a*
new (m/f)	*nuevo/a*
old (m/f)	*viejo/a*
nothing	*nada*
something (m/f)	*algo/a*
quickly	*rápidamente*
slowly (m/f)	*despacio/a*
What is this?	*¿qué es esto?*
when?	*¿cuando?*
where?	*¿dónde?*

TIME

in the afternoon, early evening	*por la tarde*
at night	*por la noche*
in the daytime	*por el día*
in the morning	*por la mañana*
minute	*minuto*
month	*mes*
ever	*jamás*
never	*nunca*
now	*ahora*
today	*hoy*
yesterday	*ayer*
tomorrow	*mañana*
What time is it?	*¿qué hora es?*
hour	*hora*
week	*semana*
year	*año*
Sunday	*domingo*
Monday	*lunes*

Tuesday	*martes*
Wednesday	*miércoles*
Thursday	*jueves*
Friday	*viernes*
Saturday	*sábado*
January	*enero*
February	*febrero*
March	*marzo*
April	*abril*
May	*mayo*
June	*junio*
July	*julio*
August	*agosto*
September	*septiembre*
October	*octubre*
November	*noviembre*
December	*diciembre*

WEATHER

It is cold	*hace frío*
It is warm	*hace calor*
It is very hot	*hace mucho calor*
sun	*sol*
It is sunny	*hace sol*
It is cloudy	*está nublado*
rain	*lluvia*
It is raining	*está lloviendo*
wind	*viento*
It is windy	*hay viento*
snow	*nieve*
damp	*húmedo*
dry	*seco*
storm	*tormenta*
hurricane	*huracán*

COMMUNICATION

air mail	*correos aéreo*
collect call	*llamada por cobrar*
dial the number	*marcar el número*
area code, country code	*código*
envelope	*sobre*
long distance	*larga distancia*
post office	*correo*
rate	*tarifa*

stamps	*estampillas*
telegram	*telegrama*
telephone book	*un guia telefónica*
wait for the tone	*esperar la señal*

ACTIVITIES

beach	*playa*
museum or gallery	*museo*
scuba diving	*buceo*
to swim	*bañarse*
to walk around	*pasear*
hiking	*caminata*
trail	*pista, sendero*
cycling	*ciclismo*
fishing	*pesca*

TRANSPORTATION

arrival	*llegada*
departure	*salida*
on time	*a tiempo*
cancelled (m/f)	*anulado/a*
one way ticket	*ida*
return	*regreso*
round trip	*ida y vuelta*
schedule	*horario*
baggage	*equipajes*
north	*norte*
south	*sur*
east	*este*
west	*oeste*
avenue	*avenida*
street	*calle*
highway	*carretera*
expressway	*autopista*
airplane	*avión*
airport	*aeropuerto*
bicycle	*bicicleta*
boat	*barco*
bus	*bus*
bus stop	*parada*
bus terminal	*terminal*
train	*tren*
train crossing	*crucero ferrocarril*
station	*estación*

neighbourhood	*barrio*
collective taxi	*colectivo*
corner	*esquina*
express	*rápido*
safe	*seguro/a*
be careful	*cuidado*
car	*coche, carro*
To rent a car	*alquilar un auto*
gas	*gasolina*
gas station	*gasolinera*
no parking	*no estacionar*
no passing	*no adelantar*
parking	*parqueo*
pedestrian	*peaton*
road closed, no through traffic	*no hay paso*
slow down	*reduzca velocidad*
speed limit	*velocidad permitida*
stop	*alto*
stop! (an order)	*pare*
traffic light	*semáforo*

ACCOMMODATION

cabin, bungalow	*cabaña*
accommodation	*alojamiento*
double, for two people	*doble*
single, for one person	*sencillo*
high season	*temporada alta*
low season	*temporada baja*
bed	*cama*
floor (first, second...)	*piso*
main floor	*planta baja*
manager	*gerente, jefe*
double bed	*cama matrimonial*
cot	*camita*
bathroom	*baños*
with private bathroom	*con baño privado*
hot water	*agua caliente*
breakfast	*desayuno*
elevator	*ascensor*
air conditioning	*aire acondicionado*
fan	*ventilador, abanico*
pool	*piscina, alberca*
room	*habitación*

SPECIAL MEXICAN TERMS

baby shark	*cazón*
bathtub	*tina*
to chat	*platicar*
chips	*totopos*
shower	*regadera*
traffic circle	*glorieta*

Please, do not bother us!   *Por favor, no mos molesta!*

NUMBERS

1	*uno*	30	*treinta*
2	*dos*	31	*treinta y uno*
3	*tres*	32	*treinta y dos*
4	*cuatro*	40	*cuarenta*
5	*cinco*	50	*cincuenta*
6	*seis*	60	*sesenta*
7	*siete*	70	*setenta*
8	*ocho*	80	*ochenta*
9	*nueve*	90	*noventa*
10	*diez*	100	*cien*
11	*once*	101	*ciento uno*
12	*doce*	102	*ciento dos*
13	*trece*	200	*doscientos*
14	*catorce*	300	*trescientos*
15	*quince*	400	*quatrocientoa*
16	*dieciséis*	500	*quinientos*
17	*diecisiete*	600	*seiscientos*
18	*dieciocho*	700	*sietecientos*
19	*diecinueve*	800	*ochocientos*
20	*veinte*	900	*novecientos*
21	*veintiuno*	1,000	*mil*
22	*veintidós*	1,100	*mil cien*
23	*veintitrés*	1,200	*mil doscientos*
24	*veinticuatro*	2000	*dos mil*
25	*veinticinco*	3000	*tres mil*
26	*veintiséis*	10,000	*diez mil*
27	*veintisiete*	100,000	*cien mil*
28	*veintiocho*	1,000,000	*un millón*
29	*veintinueve*		

INDEX

*Travel Notes*_____

*Travel Notes*_____

Travel Notes___

*Travel Notes*_____